·COTSWOLD·
MEMORIES
Recollections of Rural Life in the Steam Age

Auto train at Chipping Norton tunnel 1936
(C. R. L. Coles)

COTSWOLD MEMORIES

Recollections of Rural Life in the Steam Age

◆ RON PIGRAM · DENNIS F. EDWARDS ◆

GREENWICH EDITIONS

**Other titles by Dennis Edwards
and Ron Pigram**

Metro Memories
The Romance of Metroland
The Golden Years of the Metropolitan
    Railway
London's Underground Suburbs
The Final link

Acknowledgements

The authors would like to thank the following for their kind assistance with the illustrations and research for this book.

Cheltenham Art Gallery and
    Museums
Historical Model Society
Lens of Sutton
Oxford Publishing Company
Heyday Publishing Company
Bradford Barton
Loco and General Publishing
Oxford County Council Museum
    Services
Packer Studio
Corinium Museum, Cirencester
M. D. Shaw
S. Gardiner
University of Reading
Derek Cross

COTSWOLD MEMORIES
This edition published 1996 by
Greenwich Editions
Unit 7, 202-208 New North Road
London N1 7BJ

First published 1990

© Copyright 1990 Dennis Edwards & Ron Pigram

ISBN 0-86288-086-6

Printed and bound in Great Britain

Jacket illustration

"THE ARRIVAL" Chipping Norton in Victorian days from a modern painting by Sean Bolan

Contents

ADLESTROP

Yes, I remember Adlestrop –
The name, because one afternoon
Of heat the express-train drew up there
Unwontedly. It was late June.

The steam hissed, someone cleared his throat.
No one left and no one came
On the bare platform. What I saw
Was Adlestrop – only the name.

And willows, willow-herb, and grass,
And meadowsweet, and haycocks dry,
No whit less still and lonely fair
Than the high cloudlets in the sky.

And for that minute, a blackbird sang,
Close by, and round him, mistier,
Farther and farther, all the birds
Of Oxfordshire and Gloucestershire.

Edward Thomas

Introduction

An Aerial Reconnaissance

Come and join us on an imaginary hot-air balloon flight over the South Midlands. It is a fine sunny day and we can see for miles over some of the finest English countryside – small towns, irregular shapes and blobs of woods, stone-walled fields and meandering byways, with clusters of houses by the silvery ribbons of the streams. The wind has blown our balloon from east to west, from the red-brick of the Chilterns, then high over the golden hue of the ironstone North Oxfordshire buildings. Already we can see, from the far side of our basket, the glorious honey limestone of the Cotswolds, with the sun twinkling upon the waters of the Severn in the far distance.

From our aerial vantage point we can see the ranges of the hills which at one time were barriers to easy communication. The chalk ridges of the Chilterns, the wolds of the Cotswolds and the rough-and-tumble of the Western Edge down to the Gloucester plain. But to make our trip more interesting, and allow it to set the scene for our book, we would ask you to imagine that we are looking down on the area as it was in the early decades of this century. We can see a criss-cross of tiny lines, a pattern that weaves, links up and separates again, and forms a web, touching nearly every town and village. And little puffs of smoke – for these lines are railways. Not the great main lines, but fussy rural railways that creak and puff and clank their way through the years in much the same unhurried way as the Cotswold people live their lives.

Away to the east, as we silently float beyond Oxford, we can indeed spot a main line – the last one that was ever built from London. The Great Western Line from High Wycombe to Banbury.

On the other side, we can make out the main GWR lines from Oxford, and the string of delightful little Cotswold halts and stations that run like people towards the fruit-growing areas of Pershore, Evesham and Worcester. Everywhere, the iron road snakes around the hills, leaps the waterways and threads along the sides of the valleys.

There is the Midland & South Western Junction Railway, running north from Swindon to Cirencester and on to Cheltenham, linking with the GWR line from Banbury and Kingham at Andoversford. There are the GWR trains from Swindon to Stroud via Kemble, with the branch lines from the later place to Cirencester and Tetbury. We can see other branch lines from Oxford to Witney, Fairford and Woodstock.

Let us go down (very gently) towards the ground and have a closer look at what has been going on here during the 19th and early 20th centuries – at transport and, most important, at the people and their lives. For they provide the goods and passengers without which road and rail services would not function. We will journey from early steam days to the eve of the motorway era. It will be a long and very interesting trip to make together and we will see the changes in the social order that eventually brought about the running down of both road and rail links in the Cotswolds.

Look, a tall chimney growing rather oddly out of a dome structure lies below us. We are coming down very near Chipping Norton in Oxfordshire. Hold tight to the basket – we are about to take a step back in time . . . into a slower, quieter world, where the noise of the motor car or the bus is a rare event. Where the fields are alive with the tremulous movement of butterflies on unsprayed hedges, and the air is heavy, and warm, carrying the vague murmur of bees. Here, in the heart of the Cotswolds, a man may stand with his feet on the soil and limestone, and see the vistas before him: the line of the Wiltshire downs far to the south and the rolling landscape. He feels at peace with the sky and the earth, and across the ridge comes the sound of bleating sheep, and over to the right are fields of fresh green corn. For above all, the Cotswold landscape is one of wide skies and distant ridges. The villages hide themselves in the river valleys and the traveller will see little of them until he comes to an inviting lane, turns down it and presently passes under the trees and onto the quiet world of a village green, with its edging of limestone cottages and ancient church.

In this quiet pre-war world the things that would strike us most would be the sheer variety of the wayside flowers. Their colours and scents untainted as yet by petrol fumes and chemical sprays. The songs of the birds and the sounds of the animals. For in those days there was time to see and silence in which to listen. There were white and dusty roads, with their walls of

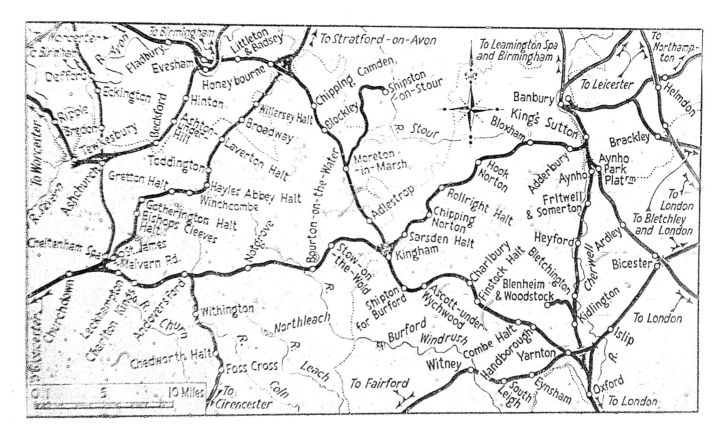

limestone and their grassy banks, winding their erratic way from village to small town. Long after the great industrial cities were made, the Cotswolds remained an unspoiled backwater.

At night, when the working hours at last came to an end with supper time, poorer families were usually in bed soon after nine. This was especially the case in winter, when the lack of good lighting and the need to conserve candles, often home made, meant that one could not read. The land workers had to get up as early as 4am to see to the herds. There was the necessity to get the milk churns to the nearest station ready for the first train of the day.

We would notice too, the silence of the roads – no roaring lorries, or cars. It was into this seemingly idyllic land that the first motor vehicles chugged their slow way before 1904. But it was after World War One that the changes really made their mark. Laurie Lee says in his classic *Cider with Rosie*:

Myself, my family, my generation, were born in a world of silence; a world of hard work and necessary patience, of backs bent to the ground, hands massaging the crops, of waiting on weather and growth; of villages like ships in the empty

Map showing the railways of the Cotswolds *c.* 1914.

landscapes and the long walking distances between them; of white narrow roads rutted by hooves and cartwheels, innocent of oil or petrol . . .

This is what we were born to, and all we knew at first. Then, to the scream of the horses, the change began. The brass-lamped motor car came coughing up the road, followed by the clamorous char-a-banc; the solid tyred bus climbed the dusty hills and more and more people came and went.

A Way of Life

The Banbury to Cheltenham railway was a somewhat winding link between some 14 village stations, and ran across the heart of the Cotswolds. There were no large towns along its route, although Chipping Norton was an important trade centre. Much of the traffic the railway carried was completely local – light industrial products, farm produce and passengers. It provided an easy way to explore the Cotswolds. The railway has gone now and the main proof of its history lies not in the occasional tumble of bricks and the remains of tunnels and viaducts, but in the memories of the older Cotswold folk still living in the area. They can tell much about the life of the 1920s and 30s.

'I never got inside a railway carriage until the day I got married,' said a middle-aged lady from the front room of her sturdy stone house at Chipping Norton. All around was the fussy collection of bric-a-brac that marks the progress of many years, each with its memories.

'I went down one day to see my cousin and met this very smart young soldier there,' she recalled. 'Who are you?' she asked him.

'I'm May's brother down the road,' the lad answered.

'What are you staring at,' she countered, 'you're a bit rude, aren't you?'

The soldier straightened himself up, 'Well,' he smiled cheekily, 'I'm only home at Norton for four days, then I'm off to India.'

'We sat up talking together until 2 o'clock in the morning, and that was something in those days, and I knew that even though I was

nineteen, my father would have a go at me. I told the soldier so.'

'In that case,' he said, 'we had better get married.'

'And we did. We were married three days later and I went to Hook Norton station to see him off. I remember that little old engine finally puffing its way around the bend to reach the station. There were quite a lot of people waiting, because the train was late. I had never been anywhere by train, but I was going up to Banbury, where he was to catch the London train. I remember getting my new dress caught in the carriage door, and everyone throwing confetti.

'We couldn't get a carriage to ourselves. The train was a Saturday one, and was quite full. We sat in a corner, looking very shy – I certainly felt so. Then, with a whistle, we were off. We moved very slowly out of Hook Norton, and I remember leaning out of the carriage and shouting to mother that I should be back on the last train.

'An old farmer and his wife in the compartment smiled and chatted to us for a bit, then left us alone. And so to Bloxham, Adderbury and on to the main line at King's Sutton. Wasn't much of a way to start a marriage, was it?' she ended.

That lady's strange honeymoon, however, does tell us quite a lot about Cotswold people. It reveals how even happy occasions had to fit in around family life and what children of those times expected from their lives. It also shows how seldom ordinary working people travelled by train.

Certainly the picture that is sometimes given of Cotswold life, with sturdy old rustics smiling through their beards from cottage gates, was different from the real situation at the turn of the century. Everyone, including children, worked long hours, and most work was monotonous and very poorly paid. At harvest time, farmhands worked until they could no longer see, and the farm milkmen had been on duty since 5am.

> Those dark nights were detested by the farm hands, the wind was like a carving knife and it cut their hands and cheeks till they bled. They wrapped mufflers round their necks when they crossed the fields, and Joshua wore mittens so that his fingers were free, but they were frozen like boards and caked with ice. (Alison Uttley).

The railways did bring some welcome steady employment, and station men tended to stay at, or near, the same station throughout their careers. Stations along the line to Chipping Norton, as well as others in the Cotswolds, had a somewhat run down, unhurried look.

In the early days of the Cotswold railways, the country folk were reluctant to use the new facilities, and when they did, it was an adventure.

> Never in my life did I go at such a rate – under and over bridges and through holes in the hills.
> J. Arthur Gibbs: *A Cotswold Village*)

There is the story of how a south Gloucestershire labourer set out by train for London. He boarded the train at Stroud and the humorous tale has it that he thought the lineside telegraph poles were for washing and that the GWR was

9

letting out the lines at a profit for drying clothes!

Transport in the Cotswolds, as with the rest of rural life, varied according to class. There was one main way of travel common to the lower classes – walking. People of all ages walked great distances, as time was of no great consequence to many. Train travel, although cheap, was still a luxury in Edwardian days. *The Diaries of George Dew*, a Cotswold Relieving Officer, tell us much about the way of life: he was what we would today call a social security worker. His job was to see if the condition of applicants for Poor Relief was really genuine and to assess what their needs were. Dew, who had wanted to become a station master and be a man of substance, had settled for Poor Law administration, which meant long hours and using his feet, with only some help from railway journeys. A typical entry in those early days went:

> *Oct. 10th:* A sharp frost last night and keen north wind this morning. Rode on the first train to the nearest station and thence to Bletchington. My business was to pay the poor. I then rode with the baker to Weston, and then walked back to my station by 6pm. If I were not so tired, and it was not so late, I could add some memoranda on the natural history of the area . . .

Dew's transport troubles were solved, for a time at least, when he was able to afford a horse – first a saddle horse, then a horse-and-trap. When he decided that he was not getting enough exercise, he sold them for a tricycle (which cost the large sum of 18 guineas), selling the pony to a 'travelling gypsy named Smith, who lives in the locality in a roadside van'.

Tricycles, and soon bicycles, were to prove a boon to most Cotswold folk. The village nurse, who did her rounds near Chipping Norton, went on her sit-up-and-beg ladies' bicycle, with its high wheels and complicated stringing from the mudguards to avoid any major disturbance of clothing. The single horse trap (or 'dog cart') that Mr Dew had used was quickly to become the family 'runabout' or 'mini' of Edwardian days. Many could be seen, with smartly dressed

young ladies at the whip, awaiting the evening train from Kingham or Banbury for their fathers returning from business. In those days, of course, most of the travellers were men, women retaining their traditional role as housewives.

Outside the stations the roads wound dustily away, climbing between hedges and tall grass, with here and there a glimpse of a limestone wall: each stone carefully balanced on another and no mortar used. In those years there was above all, an overriding silence, especially on Sundays, when many railways observed 'church times' till around midday and no trains ran. Not that it was thought that the trains disturbed worshippers, but it allowed staff to attend a place of worship.

Early morning on the Over Norton road just outside Chipping Norton in the 1900s.

Over the fields one might have caught a glimpse of a plough team at work in the autumn; or in late summer, the harvesters at work and the sound of the thrashing machine driven by a chugging steam engine, the smell of steam and oil drifting over the fields. Then there was the chinking horse harness and the crunch of iron tyres on the gravel roads and the clop of the horses. But these were the only sounds in the countryside then. At the station, between trains, the platforms slept in the sunshine or brooded under the heavy drizzle. Frequently at night, the only lights amid the rural darkness were those of the station

West End, Northleach.

Northleach
The railways did not reach anywhere near the old wool town of Northleach and, with the end of the stage coach trade, the highway from Oxford to Cheltenham lay quiet and seldom disturbed. Yet thirty years after this view, it was becoming busy again with early motor traffic.

Reflections
The two oldest people in Sibford at the turn of the century. The years are marked on their faces. Most women appeared to have dressed in black at an early age; perhaps reflecting the death rate at the time.

George Dew, a Cotswold Relieving Officer in the 1880s and 1900s, made many trips by railway and dog-cart around the villages, confining some elderly people to the attentions of the Workhouse Keepers, or occasionally paying the poor a tiny sum which they were able to use for bread. Every effort was made to avoid carrying too many of the poor on the parish, but most would starve rather than face workhouse disgrace.

Potato Planting
Here a boy shows how the potatoes were placed separately into this hand-wheeled planter on a Cotswold Farm at Lower Slaughter. It must have required a great effort to push it over the ploughed land.

Harvest Home
Another farm scene in the Cotswolds near Banbury about 1904. Progress was being made in the mechanisation of harvest machinery. This farm has its reapers-binders on show, with complete fields of cut corn visible in the distance. The harvest seems to be almost over, and the smiles of satisfaction on the faces of many of the farmhands may be in anticipation of the general merrymaking and drinking to come when all was gathered in. Note the crowd of small boys who could club down rabbits trapped in the corn.

buildings and the signal lamps. The station staff occupied their time by keeping the premises clean, and cultivating the station gardens, or stoking the fires in bleak January.

Everybody for miles around knew the times of the trains and, some ten minutes before a train was due, a wagon and horses would appear with the milk churns; a couple of cyclists next, dismounting from their tall and sturdy machines. Then a governess cart with a couple of fine, high-stepping horses, waiting to meet somebody important coming for the weekend at the big house. The station staff stirred themselves and got the parcels ready. The arm of the signal would clank down and the rails begin to vibrate. A plume of steam would rise over the far distant bridge. Then the train came into sight – perhaps a 'Metro' tank and some clerestory carriages, or in the 1920s, a 'Prairie' tank and a brace of 'B' set carriages, or one of the 0-6-0 locomotives propelling its auto-carriage, the driver at the controls in the front of the long and antique-looking saloon carriage.

At the more important stations,

like Kingham or Moreton-in-Marsh, the express trains might stop on their journeys from London, or cross-country from perhaps Newcastle to Wales. The well dressed passengers in the First Class, would be taking tea as the green Cotswold countryside passed by the windows. Outside the stations, the roads before the days of tarmac, were fit only for the carriers' carts and wagons, which plied from village to village at certain fixed times of the week. They carried room for passengers amid the piles of goods that had to be dropped off at farms on the route. It was only in the early 1920s that the motor bus became a threat to the Cotswold railways. Of course, the local gentry had experimented with the 'motor' from Edwardian times. But then every working man and woman had agreed that the way of the gentry was a strange and different world from their own, even though they all lived near each other.

'I don't know what they got up to, up at the Hall,' was a comment heard even in recent days. The Almighty, in those great days of Church and Chapel, had separated

The milkman gets through
Despite the appalling weather, the milkman struggles amid the snow which covered Chipping Norton market place one winter day in 1931. Milk was sold from the churn via a scoop and milk can at this time.

the classes. No-one envied the gentleman's place in the order of things. They were just 'different' and did different things, such as hunting.

It was only when the working classes of rural communities started to become more prosperous at the start of the car age – during the 1950s that rural transport systems, which had structured so much of Cotswold life, with links between villages and towns, began to break down. It did so quite rapidly, and the Cotswold branch lines and minor cross-country railways were abandoned within a decade. A process of re-adjustment that interplayed with the other factors of the agricultural way of life – small breweries, chair-making, cloth manufacture, light engineering and other crafts, and the products of the land itself. For all had once been transported by train or lorry to the station.

The Threshing Machine

This picture, which appears to date from the late 1890s could have been taken on most Cotswold farms where corn (wheat) was grown. The very early steam tractor with its tall chimney, drives a languid belt to the box-like thresher, the beaten grain being collected in sacks placed in position near the ladder.

This operation was the most unpleasant of the harvest tasks. Farms waited for their turn for the threshing machine to arrive (most were run by farm contractors). Once on the farm, time was vital, and the intense amounts of dust from the flailed wheat, oats or barley would give rise to large and continuous amounts of filth. The machine operations, moreover, were far from safe as this picture may indicate. Finally, the hands were in danger of rat bites from the rodents who burrowed into the standing stacks of cereal, which had to be forked into the hoppers.

Country Society

The Well-to-Do

Although many Cotswold Houses have origins that go back many centuries (Snowshill, Sudley etc) the 19th century witnessed a considerable increase in large houses for successful manufacturers and tradesmen. They were able to take a train from near their country estates in the Cotswolds to the cities where they controlled great companies. Railways from Banbury, Oxford, Cirencester and Cheltenham were more numerous in Edwardian days than at any time before or since. The gentry found that they were allowed to merge quickly into the well-practised routine of the Cotswold country life, as long as they observed the rather rigid rules by which it was governed.

Most country houses and mansions erected during Victorian and Edwardian times were on a grand scale, and such ostentation was looked upon by the established gentry as the first sign of respectability. But there were critics and in the 1880s many of the new gentry were called 'Jumped-up Jubilee Knights' by the more vocal members of the farming community.

As soon as the new arrivals had had time to settle in, the local persons of equal standing would regard it as a necessary courtesy for a 'call' to be made, as a gesture of welcome. The visiting card appeared with this formality, and one young girl during Edwardian times, Miss Lewis, writing of her memories years later, recalled that she and her mother would set out in a dog-cart in their best clothes, the mother secretly hoping that they would find no one at home, so that the visiting card, with its invitation to formal tea could be left without having to spend the whole afternoon with complete strangers, people who usually had so much more to show in wealth than they had. It was easier to entertain these newcomers in one's own house.

The visiting card rule was one of many curious practices of the period, practices that included a way of dealing with children in which the child had to wait outside the drawing room after telling the servant that they wished to be allowed to enter. If they were, they had to sit down and keep upright, not 'lolling' or allowing their legs to swing. A similar old practice was found in the Oxford publication *The Rule of Civility* (1671) and dealt with sneezing:

> 'We must not cry out "God Bless You!" with any considerable address, but pull off our hat, make our reverence, and speak that benediction to ourselves.'

If the newcomers returned the visiting card, an exchange of visits to dinner or tea would take place, after which they were usually accepted into the local country pursuits of the gentry – including hunting and shooting, the latter sport being tremendously popular and increasingly lethal (for the game birds) during the first 30 years of the present century, with the increase in the efficiency of firearms. Thousands of game birds were massacred during weekend visits to large Cotswold estates. Edward VII, of course, really set the fashion for the weekend visit – a descent upon a local landowner that called for stringent planning by everyone at the house concerned, including the maids who were forced to give up some of their rooms for the large groups of servants that accompanied the visitors. The arrival of such royal parties required the collection of much luggage sent in advance to the nearest railway station, to be collected and brought up to the house.

The ordinary staff of such houses were recruited with ease from the local girls of the nearby villages. Boys, too, were drawn into domestic service for awhile, and were then passed into various rural crafts and trades, often continuing to work for these wealthy employers. Wages were poor, but such work often provided the only local source of employment for the rapidly increasing population of the Cotswold villages. Many people were lured away to try their luck in far-off London, or some other large centre. In such a way, the 'big' house did give some stability to Cotswold village life at this time.

Into this slowly changing world came the motor car, a plaything of the rich for some years. Much esteem could be gained if important weekend visitors, especially royal ones, could be met by one of the new 'motors'. King Edward had a great love of travelling by these experimental monsters.

All early cars were hand-made, based on the principle of the horse-drawn coach (hence 'coachwork') and were prone to many breakdowns because of the unreliability of the engine and mechanical parts and from tyre damage in an age of uncoated highways. A drive in one of these early motors was not a very pleasant experience, but at least the riders were the centre of attraction. The vibration alone could be heavily felt and the motion over even slightly undulating surfaces set up a side-to-side motion, as well as a forward one, creating conditions that could make the motorist rather queezy. Perhaps it was just as well that most vehicles were open in those days!

One of the main reasons why the early motor bus had such a fitful birth was the problem of tyres, and nowhere was it felt more than in the Cotswold byways. Tyres had a habit of simply coming off the rim when subjected to continuous oscillating motion, forcing buses off the road and making the private motorist liable to constant delays.

The new form of road transport required a new type of servant – the chauffeur, to look after it in the same way that the brougham or fly required a horseman/handyman to keep the drawing animals in good condition. Mr William Coombes recalled his early days as a chauffeur for a titled gentleman near Banbury, as times of constant improvisation, in which he was forced to undertake work normally done by a blacksmith and carpenter. 'You had to be a Jack-of-all-trades then.'

With this in mind, it was essential for the prospective chauffeur to be a handyman as well. This was brought home to one employer forcibly when he broke down some miles away from his home. He was driving himself, and such an occurrence usually meant a tow home by a local horseman, to the delight of the villagers en route. However, as he stood outside surveying the heavy list that his vehicle had suddenly developed, a young man passing by said that he could see the trouble right away – one of the large 'pram' springs that coiled away to support the rear of the car had broken. Without more ado, this enterprising young man unbolted the two pieces of the spring, and set off to the nearest blacksmith's forge, where he was

allowed to join the broken pieces together again, and refix them to the car. This was to earn him not only a sovereign, but the position of chauffeur.

Young men returning from the front after the First War sought these high-status domestic positions; many had picked up some knowledge of how engines worked, or were simply not excited, by the thought of returning to the fields as simple farm hands, even if there was enough work to be found. The new chauffeur-mechanic soon became a popular member of the household staff – especially among the young girls, maids and the young 'misses' of the establishment. These men cut a romantic figure – they could be relied upon at breakdowns to get the car moving somehow, and some illustrations from the cartoons of the times show the young 'misses' playing badminton beside the road whilst waiting for the chauffeur to finish under the car bonnet.

Chauffeurs were firmly kept in their place by the older generation who, by and large, did not hold with cars. A delightful book of the 1920s was entitled *Home, James!* and gave some insight into the origin of the term. It appears that most employers called their chauffeurs by their surnames, but one lady, about to appoint a man for the first time, was rather taken aback when he told her that his name was 'Darling, James Darling'. Obviously he could not be called by anything but his Christian name, so 'Home, James' it was. This little book gave hints on correct etiquette when dealing with motoring visitors; a chauffeur's responsibilities, and the need to be ready at all times to have the car 'brought round'.

William Coombes, mentioned earlier, indicated that to tackle a lengthy ride in the early 1920s from the Cotswolds near Banbury to Devon, called for much preparation. After any trip, even a mile or so, he recalls, he made it standard practice to remove the wheels from the Rolls Royce and clean underneath. For long journeys extra sets of tyres were often carried.

'Petrol,' said Coombes 'was another headache in those days. There were very few petrol stations. You were lucky if there was any pump at all in quite large towns, or so it seemed. We carried a supply of petrol at the house, and I always put extra cans in the car.' The fuel was delivered in drums, and often the liquid was fed out into the car by a sort of hand-pump arrangement. There were some familiar and unfamiliar brand names. National Benzole Mixture was advertised in the 1930s as well as Shell. But there were cheaper supplies from places like Russia: ROP, Russian Oil Products, was one such brand. As more and more cars were seen on the roads, petrol supplies improved. Early advertising by National Benzole featured a well-groomed woman driving an open car being seduced by a metallic-looking youth – the 'god of the roads' who always whispered that the reason for her smooth driving was the presence of the benzole additive.

Another old chauffeur recalled how his car ran out of petrol deep in the Cotswolds near Stanway. Surprisingly, a woman came out from a nearby cottage and asked if he wanted petrol, and then brought a supply in a number of cans. It appeared that she had decided to hold petrol supplies in this primitive and dangerous way because she foresaw the demand, and was about to erect a sign announcing 'Motor Spirit Sold Here'.

Not every one wanted a limousine. The children of the large houses learned to drive using little 'runabout' cars such as the Bean, a 4-seater selling in the 20s for £345. The company, A. Harper and Sons and Bean of Dudley, Worcestershire, also sold a 2-seater which was much more fun, for only £335. This was still a colossal amount of money for the time. The 2-seater had a 'dicky', a rear seat that was encased out of sight, rather like a boot, but which could be pressed down to allow the seat to appear – a snug romantic place, where intimate hugs and kisses could be enjoyed out in the open air, even if father and mother were in the front of the vehicle!

Life in the Cotswold country

house was little affected by the motor car for many years. During the early part of this century it was still the practice to keep the family brougham, along with any cars, in some outhouse. With rising costs, however, the horse which drew the brougham would also be expected to be used for a number of ancillary carriages and sometimes even for pulling the huge lawn mower!

The annual holiday was another great event in the year for these people. The whole house would be closed down, apart from a very small staff to service the animals and essentials. When the family was about to return again, covers were removed from furniture and ornaments, and maids set to with a vengeance, starting very early in the morning and working around the clock as the farm labourers did. In those days, before modern electrical heating, fires had to be laid and lit in most rooms and the ashes cleared away again next morning. Brushes and mops were the tools of the day, although by 1908 the first vacuum cleaners were starting to appear in the more advanced households. Lack of

electricity in many places, particularly the Cotswolds, meant oil or candle lighting. Washing of clothes was carried out by coal fired coppers and much hard hand work.

Some of the big houses eventually installed generators. 'At our house,' recalled Mrs. Lewis in her book *Life in a Country House*, 'we ran an electrical generator which ran from an engine. This machine, which burned oil, was housed in an outhouse. The mechanic, after decarbonising the family car, had to prime the generator engine by means of a blow lamp, then swing the huge flywheel which drove the belt. The brass governor would start to rise and glint in the sun, the spokes of the flywheel would cease to stand distinct, but blurred into diffusion as the speed mounted.'

The outdoor staff at big houses was employed in large numbers. Huge greenhouses brought plenty of exotic fruit to the dining room table, with grapes being a special prize. Black Hambergs were first in the season, while later Madresfield grapes were brought in. Most households were firmly of

the idea that to swallow a grape pip would bring on appendicitis, so children were trained to retain the pip on their tongue-tips and eject them with care to the side of their plates. It was all part of learning to be a lady or gentleman.

Miss Lewis also gives us, in her book, an idea of the food consumed daily by the big houses in the Cotswolds. A weekday breakfast would have consisted of eggs, bacon, kippers, haddock, fish cakes or kidneys. This kind of fare was a stable part of the menu in railway dining cars until quite recent days. Sunday lunch was the traditional roast beef with sometimes chicken or mutton. The remains of this provided cold meat for Monday lunch.

Dinner was always a grand affair. The women wore fine gowns and covered their shoulders with shawls or stoles – vital if they were

17

seated far from the fire. The men dressed in black suits with black bow ties, although by the inter-war years it became permissible for a softer version of the stiff evening shirt to be worn. At the dinners, the soup was ladled out by the butler into red-hot plates and handed round the table by the maids. Some houses, like Blenheim Palace, would have footmen for this purpose. Fish, grouse, partridges or pheasants formed the bill of fare, and there were usually menu cards written out and stuck in holders at each table or near each place. Afterwards, the children were encouraged to leave for bed with the Nanny in charge. It was all very English – correct and unchanging. Any scandal affecting the family was, as far as possible, retained within the strict family circle, although the drawbacks of having servants was their 'tittle-tattle' and their prying eyes.

Edwardian decorum
A garden party held in the grounds of the Manse at France Lynch Methodist Chapel, Chalford.

Royal Welcome at Chipping Norton
King Edward VII was Proclaimed on Tuesday 29 January 1901. Most town dignitaries considered how the Coronation could best be celebrated. The South African War was drawing to a close and people were in the mood for rejoicing.

Sadly, the King was taken ill at the time when arrangements were almost complete, and hurried work behind the scenes throughout the country was necessary to defer the happy day until Saturday 9 August 1902, some months after the original planned date.

However, it did mean that people could celebrate in the middle of summer, as this massed public lunch in the centre of Chipping Norton shows. Few places of their size could have surpassed this enormous spread!

The Working Class and the Cotswold Scene

It was a different story in the early 1900s for the people who lived in the run-down cottages – those people who provided labour for working the farms and estates. There was, of course, as has already been said, no electricity for most of the Cotswolds, and no piped water. One of the earliest installations was at Blockley. The Rushout family provided the village with power in 1880, the generator being worked by a dam specially built across a local stream. But in the average Cotswold cottage, life went on in the same living room that had been used by the family for generations and the only lighting in the evenings was by oil lamp. The food was spartan, and a great delicacy was the pork from the annual killing of the family pig. The flesh was smoked in the chimney, and hung from the ceiling to 'cure'.

But by the end of the nineteenth century, the lot of the rural population in the Cotswolds was at a low ebb.

A book called *How the Labourer Lives*, appeared about the same time as a damaging report in the British Medical Journal (1903) on the state of health of the Cotswold working man. The wife of a farm labourer remarked, 'The shoes I can get never come straight from the shops.' It was reference to her attempts to try to clothe her growing children, differing in age as well as sex. On the London streets, children could get along without any shoes, but something was needed in the fields.

Mrs. Pember Reeves' *Round About a Pound a Week*, which appeared in 1913, dwelt on overcrowding in country cottages.

> In one room will sleep father, mother and baby, while on another bed will sleep the four other children. Often the lodger-granny will take a child into her bed, or the lodger-uncle will take one of the boys. The four-in-a-bed arrangement was common enough to want attention.

There were plenty of people, all well off, prepared to tour around the villages and comment. General Booth's Salvation Army appealed in the country as well as the towns, for these were the days when drink was seen as the major cause of social misery. However, Booth himself could be blinkered at times: 'I see nothing improbable in the general view that the simple natural lives of working-class farm labourers tend to their own and their children's happiness more than the artificial complicated existence of the rich.'

Still, as we have seen, there was a growing sense of awareness of the problem of poverty. One lady from a well-to-do background and showing an interest in the problem of rural poverty, asked the wife of a labourer near Stow-on-the-Wold:

'But how *do* you live?'

'I couldn't tell you how we do live, ma'am,' replied the rather dazed woman, 'I don't know how we do manage; the thing is to get it *past*.'

But it was not all graft; the village people were capable of helping each other and enjoying themselves. For the men, this often meant the local pub, but for the children and young people, amusements were very simple and mostly free.

'On Sundays, a lot of us girls would go for a walk,' Ann Stevens of Steeple Ashton remembered. 'There were twelve or more of us, mostly arm in arm, going through the gates into the fields and admiring the daisies. They would think you were daft today.'

She recalled that gangs of the village lads would be seen on a summer's night grouped around the doorways, keeping an eye open for the local girls.

Travel to local fairs was a popular pastime in summer and autumn. One fête in Blenheim Park in 1902, in aid of the GWR Widow and Orphan Fund, brought excursion trains from all parts of the region to the terminus at Woodstock, right opposite the park gates.

In *The Diaries of George Dew*, the Relieving Officer we have mentioned before, is a note on the popularity of the country fair:

> *October 17th* Very gay day at Bicester, being a fair day. Fairs although formerly of much consequence as places of resort, have since the introduction of railways, lost much of their importance and popularity. There were a number of servant girls walking about, but in late years they have so altered in their style of dress that it is difficult to judge as to mistress and servant! There was a large wooden wax-work show, but the greatest novelty to me was the horses (wooden) and carriages which were driven round by a Steam Engine, while another small engine, which worked without cessation, drove an organ, both engines (one boiler) were very nicely made and must have cost a large sum of money. I paid a penny

to see a 'show' of performing birds. They had a very small dwarf (man) which interested me very much.

Throughout the century, the travelling fair has brought this sense of harmless fun to the Cotswolds; a typical site is that of Chipping Norton, where annually the fair apparatus is still somehow crammed into the limited area above the main road. There is also a street fair at Stow.

Young country people tried to look as grown up as possible on these festive occasions. Fancy ties, bows and, surprisingly, socks, were regarded by boys we would now call 'teenagers', as extremely important – perhaps because these low-cost items could change appearances quickly. Boys gathering at these country fairs liked to sit on the grass and pull their trouser legs up a little to allow everyone to see their socks! Hats were very important to every man – at least for the first 30 or so years of the twentieth century. It was thought that in a curious way, to leave the head exposed was to court trouble through over-exposure to the harmful rays of the sun. However, caps and hats were of use to keep in body warmth in an age before central heating, and

most photographs of the times show a slavish devotion to headwear. It was an unofficial symbol of class – the upper class using top-hats; the middle class bowlers (later the trilby) and the working man enjoying the comfort of his cap. These caps were often set by young men at a rakish angle, when circulating at fêtes and fairs and such social opportunities. Mr. Hearn, a pensioner of Charlbury, told us, 'At 17 it was important to look as much of a man as possible.'

Sometimes visits were made to the market towns to have tea with relatives, and all kinds of country delicacies were prepared and taken along as gifts. Best clothes were worn and as described in *Lark Rise to Candleford*:

> Candleford seemed a very large and grand place to Lauria, with its several streets meeting in a square – a space where there were many large shop windows with their blinds drawn down because it was Sunday, and a doctor's house with a red lamp over the gate and a church with a tall spire, and women and girls in light summer frocks and men in smart suits and white straw boater-shaped hats . . .

Bank holidays were great occasions for the country working

Burford Hiring Fair 1895
Hiring fairs enabled the domestic employers to seek staff help, either about the house or the farm. This English way of taking on casual labour was dying out at the end of the nineteenth century, although casual dock labour was hired in this way for many years afterwards. Here the main street is lined with a variety of tiny stalls, lending a carnival atmosphere. There is no hint of the severe traffic problems that exist in the town today.

class, who seized the opportunity to join one of the many railway excursions to reach Oxford for perhaps a day by the river. Other favourite destinations were Gloucester, Stratford, or Cheltenham, whilst the more moneyed joined special trains for some far-away seaside resort. For many years the proprietors of the local newspaper in Stroud organised an annual special train to take their employees and friends to the sea or some other resort. Later they extended the sales of tickets to the public.

On Sundays and Bank Holidays the young men and women walked out in their 'Sunday best' and enjoyed themselves, in what was known as the 'monkey parade', perhaps from the elaborately dressed monkeys that perched

upon the hurdy-gurdies of the vagrant organ-grinders who were to be seen in most market towns.

By the late 1920s many towns had a cinema or at least a public hall in which films mights be shown. The cinema brought a new sort of enjoyment to those able to afford the few coppers necessary for a seat in the dark. It was still a major cost to a farm lad earning less that 10 shillings (50p) a week, but at least the cinema brought privacy.

Mrs. James Coggins, an elderly Cotswold lady told us about her first visit by train to Banbury where she went to a cinema with her girl friends in the autumn of 1929:

'I knew that I was attractive, but I didn't dwell on it. I worked as a parlour maid, and one of my friends told me about her visit to the cinema. When I got inside, some boys started to whistle. I was amazed as it was so dark. There was so many people inside. I couldn't believe it. Then the film – I didn't know what it was, but some girl near me was crying as she watched. Mum was so cross with me for being late home that she knocked me down.'

Stroud excursion
For many years, the proprietors of the *Stroud News* took their employees and friends on an annual outing, hiring a special train. Apparently some tickets were also available for the public. The last time the special train was run was in 1924 for the British Empire Exhibition at Wembley.

The Farm Economy

For those who got married, life in the Cotswolds, as in most English country communities, meant long hours of hard work. For the women it meant endless child rearing, and doing odd jobs such as scrubbing or washing to get a little extra money. For the men on the farms there was the harshness of working through the natural seasons with rather primitive machinery. Steam ploughing had arrived during the middle years of the nineteenth century. Edward Bowly of Cirencester wrote in the 1880s that steam threshing had 'become common in the last ten years.' The machines trundled from farm to farm in the threshing season, as did the companion steam engines, travelling in slow lumbering convoys. The machines were owned by firms of specialists such as F. & W. Chew of Tetbury or John and Thomas Jefford of Moreton-in-Marsh and Chipping Campden.

Even in the age of petrol, the steam engines continued to puff their versatile power deep in the fields, turning belts for the balers pressing the hay for winter feed, or in farmyards: panting in dirty gasps of smoke when geared to the threshers. In fact, the Cotswolds were an area where steam farm equipment was extensively used.

Steam ploughing, where two steam engines were used to draw a plough connected by a wire hawser to a winch and pulley, sometimes caused concern. The farmer would often set the machines just behind the hedge that lined a country lane, so that as little headland as possible was left unploughed. An indignant 'gentlewoman' of Cheltenham wrote to her local newspaper in October 1897:

> Sir, it is disgraceful the way that our lives are put at risk during innocent excursions around the countryside in dog-carts or on horseback, by farmers using steam too close to the roads. My horse bolted the other day as a loud roar of steam was released from such an engine located just beyond the road, causing my life to be put in peril, until it was restrained by a helpful gentleman a full half-mile away. What is England coming to?

But although steam ploughing died out, it was the custom until the Second World War for steam engines with solid tyres to be used by contractors around the farms. They were also used for the transport of limestone from the many small quarries which could be found throughout the Cotswold hills.

After a long day's work, there was often little to do in an age before wireless or television. Newspapers were seldom bought and even if they were, the master of the house often kept them from the women-folk and the children. Outside world events were little talked about and even less the world of Art and Literature. When Oscar Wilde was on trial, the men of the village had their newspapers hidden from the family. The family would retire early to bed to save oil.

When they were able, the men of the family would walk or cycle to the local pub for some companionship and a game of darts. The 'evils of drink' were feared most by 'do-gooders' in the countryside: it was seen as being the cause of an honest man failing to provide bread for his family. On some occasions drink could lead to an early death, as Mr. Charles Faulkner, Coroner for Heyford in Oxfordshire found on 27th July 1878 at an inquest on William Tackley. Tackley was a railway plate-layer who was killed near Cleeve Bridge at Lower Heyford on the Great Western Railway. Sometime after 10.30pm, the jury was told, he was walking towards his home in an advanced state of intoxication through an excess of alcohol. The body was found next morning with a smashed shoulder and a very severe scalp wound. He left a widow and five young children

Most men cultivated their gardens or an allotment in the village in an attempt to be self-sufficient, and most kept chickens or a pig if there was room. For those that failed, poverty was all-embracing. It meant, until the end of the 1930s, detention in the local workhouse under conditions of great privation which had their origin in the early 19th century ethics of people like the Rev. H. H. Milman:

> The workhouse should be a place of hardship, of course fair, of degradation and humility; it should be administered with strictness – with severity, it should be as repulsive as is consistent with humanity.

No wonder that many independent spirits preferred a life on the open road as a tramp, sleeping under the hedgerows or barns, and using their wits to earn, beg or steal a penny for those essentials of life, tea, beer and baccy.

Off to the mill

Two delightful studies from the camera of Frank Packer of Chipping Norton. They were entitled 'Off to the mill old style and new style'. The wagons have an extra horse in order to handle about the same amount as the two farm wagons. There was probably little difference in speed. Considerable savings can be made by farmers, even today, by taking their barley or wheat direct to the corn merchants.

Ploughing with oxen
Few of us will have seen oxen yoked to the hand-plough and it appears that, even when this picture was taken in the early 1900s the use of oxen was fast dying out. The horse had improved in strength and the ox-teams required two men each. Oxen were used for their strength, giving rise to our saying 'as strong as an ox'.

Steam on the farm
Even as late as 1948 it was possible to see this Marshall Portable Engine at work on a farm near Witney.

Commerce

In our age of supermarkets, we sometimes forget the revolution in our food purchasing since the 1950s. England, and certainly the Cotswolds, was indeed a nation of small shopkeepers and the village shop was as much a social centre as a necessary part of the housewife's day. Houses were less densely packed and the community was spread out. In most cases in the farms and hamlets people baked their own bread and grew their own vegetables. With so much dairy produce around them, the country wives usually relied upon milk either brought home in a small can by their farm worker husbands or sons, or from the farm along the road. To provide other weekday essentials, a tradesman's horse and cart could be seen in most communities once a week. Near the villages and farms, families would be 'waited on daily'. The mobile shop was quite vital: it could bring fresh meat or oil for the lamps. Henry Weston and Sons, a Chipping Norton butcher, 'purveyed' in a large delivery van, rather like a hearse, to surrounding villages, including Churchill and Kingham in the 1920s. Another travelling trade was that of hardware – everything from tin baths (for the very occasional family wash) to pots and cooking pans, soap and mops. These products were often festooned from the roof of this type of van.

The bicycle was widely used for local town deliveries, and an adaptation of this in the form of a tricycle to deliver milk from cans was a familiar sight, the milk being ladled out as required.

Hygiene regulations eventually put an end to this kind of milk sale after the Second World War.

The traditional village shop was not just a grocery store. It usually combined the post office as well as selling gardening tools, clothing, sewing materials, boots and shoes – in fact everything from a thimble to a packet of aniseed balls. When the age of cyclists came, village shops began selling light refreshments and even offering cycle repairs. The inter War years were perhaps the high day of the village store. Cut flowers, cream teas and guide books, sepia coloured post cards and home made cakes were sold to the town motorist – and some shops even sold petrol.

But above all, the village shop was a social centre. Important local gossip was exchanged, notices displayed of flower shows and garden fêtes; items for sale and coach outings to the seaside. Cars and supermarkets have changed all that and in the last ten years the number of Cotswold village shops has dropped dramatically.

There were some specialist shops for ladies, which sold millinery and dressmaking materials. These were sited in larger towns such as Cirencester. Such large shops were delights for children, as many used an overhead system for cash, in which the customer's money and bill were placed in a wooden cup shaped container, inserted into a wheeled holder on an overhead rail and wireway and then catapulted to the cashier's desk, hidden away in the dark depths at the rear of the establishment.

Most Cotswold towns have markets and in the old days they were primarily for selling live animals. Stow, perhaps, had the largest, whilst smaller towns like Lechlade had very small affairs and catered only for local needs. General markets, too, brought many people into town, and it is true to say that much of the rough-and-tumble of those days before 1939 has now been lost. So many of the market characters have disappeared. One such trader was the candy man, who provided much free entertainment, especially for children, as he made his sweets by pulling the striped confection over a large steel hook on his stall with great rapidity. After several pulls the stuff began to change colour from brown to cream. Then it would be put through a small 'mangle' which cut it into small squares. Sometimes there were free samples, but all were assured that the concoction would cure all coughs and colds, asthma and bronchitis, and all complaints of the throat, chest and lungs!

Another amusing trader was the china-stall operator. There was at least one to be seen at every market in Gloucestershire and Oxfordshire. As the proprietor rattled his plates and dishes, he kept up a running commentary that was sometimes quite ribald and therefore of great appeal to down-to-earth Cotswold folk.

In those days when most cottagers had to make their own amusements, the piano or violin could be found in many families. The musical side of things was

Can you spare a penny?
The traveller often met with the poor along the Cotswold roads after the First World War. Wandering groups of ex-servicemen were always to be found, sometimes singing for a few coppers in the village streets, or playing screeching records of Harry Lauder and Dame Clara Butt on portable clockwork gramophones. This 'disc jockey' waits, cap in hand, for an offering from the photographer. Note the pile of stones behind him, used for road repairs, as well as the early travelling grocer's van.

Mr Atkinson, The Corn Merchant
Every household kept chickens and often the family pig – all slaughtered in a primitive fashion by one of the family or a travelling butcher. Corn and seed were important to farmers. There was always a pleasant country odour about the shop, the milled products giving up an aroma which somehow lingered and aroused *Lark Rise to Candleford* memories.

Money on the hoof
Sheep rearing was the mainstay of the wealth of the Cotswolds in mediaeval times, and was still important until the agricultural slumps of the 1880s and 1930s, when so many farmers went bankrupt. There was still a healthy local market here at Chipping Norton in 1911, when this photograph was taken. Note the early petrol sign, hastily painted on an outrigger from the wall of a local cycle shop.

26

Market day

Another view of the market, looking east. A drove of donkeys and ponies awaits buyers. The local shop is not being out done and has placed its stock of agricultural machinery and mashers on street display. This was essentially a practice from before the First World War for the indigenous rural population were quite honest.

A dip in the river

Scene on the Thames near Radcot Bridge (1885). The sheep are being dipped in the open river rather than a narrow sheep dip filled with disinfectant solution. Sheep are dipped against blowfly and other pests which could infect the fleece. The Thames provided a convenient washing place. In modern times proper washing equipment would be used in the farmyard.

A Cotswold blacksmith and farrier

A farmhorse gets a new pair of shoes at this country forge in Milton-under-Wychwood.

also catered for at street markets by a stall equipped with a piano or pianola. The latter played the 'latest hits' from rolls of punched paper tapes. On a 'live' piano the latest music hall tunes would be played from sheet music costing as much as 6d (2½p) per copy. In 1912, after Lloyd George's 'Nine Pence for Four Pence' National Insurance Scheme, a pianist at Witney market was heard to sing:

Oh Lloyd George, now we're all employed
In this little island we were born in
Now everyone but tramps have got to lick the stamps,
And stick them on their cards on Friday morning.

Most market stall holders illuminated their wares at night by gas lamps which produced a bright glare and a continuous hiss. The lamps threw over all faces a yellow light, somehow a warming glow that helped to crowd the customers together on wet winter afternoons. Some stalls sold paraffin, firewood and creosote. The wood was cut from old railway sleepers and then tied into bundles by the tramps from the local workhouse, who were required to do some hard work in exchange for a roof over their heads for the night. The bundles cost 3d (just over 1p).

Cross-country bus
Early poster advertising connecting bus service in the eastern Cotswolds.

The Country Bus

Early in the twentieth century, the main way of reaching the country towns was by railway, the alternative being a ride by carrier's cart, bicycling or walking. However, there were some rural horse-bus services in Victorian days – mainly as 'feeders' to the railways. Arthur Gibbs in his *A Cotswold Village* describes how he rode the bus from Bampton on the Fairford branch line, northwards, to the then remote town of Burford. The period was the 1890s. Apparently the bus started from what he called 'Bampton-in-the-Bush' and was 'a rickety old bus.' The fare was as much as 1/- (5p):

We were soon slowly traversing the white limestone road, stopping every now and then to set down a passenger or deposit a parcel at some clean-looking, stone-faced cottage in the straggling old villages.

It was indeed, a glorious morning for an expedition into the Cotswolds. The six weeks drought had just given place to cool, showery weather. A light wind from the west breathed the fragrance of countless wild flowers and sweet may blossom from the hedges, and the scent of roses and honeysuckle was wafted from every cottage garden.

How idyllic it all sounds! Yet how bumpy and dusty the journey must have been. In winter or autumn, with the rain pouring down, making the roads like slippery porridge, it could have been a dangerous trip, too. Gibbs writes that Burford was at last reached along 'empty dusty highways' and that the bus pulled up in an almost ghostly, quiet high street.

The garden-seat type horse-drawn bus was a common sight in the streets and suburbs of towns like Oxford, Cheltenham and Banbury. Well into the present century these buses were also giving service along the main country roads.

By the early 1920s petrol buses were beginning to link the Cotswold villages and towns. The buses were usually single deck and often had provision on the roof for large items of baggage. There were no 'official' bus stops in the modern sense. One just stopped the bus by holding out an arm or waving anywhere along the country road.

The main hazard of early motor bus travel was a steep hill. Any slope of more than 1 in 8 was usually beyond the capacity of these early vehicles. When there was any doubt about the bus's ability to climb the hill, the male passengers were requested to alight and walk up behind. The bus would grind slowly up the incline, often with steam emitting from the radiator cap. At the summit the men would board the bus and after waiting a couple of minutes for the engine to cool, the bus would proceed on its journey.

Another feature of many of these early buses was the seat arrangement – two rows behind the driver. Like the driving position itself, they could often be placed outside the main body of the bus, and open at the front (there was no windscreen), though often the projecting roof of the vehicle gave some uncertain protection against the worst of the weather. These outside seats were much sought after during the summer.

When open-top double deckers appeared, they were much higher powered and could dispense with passenger assistance on hills. But passengers still held their breath as the driver went through his gear box as they ascended, with the bus almost stationary as he sought to engage the bottom gear near the summit.

Of course, there were accidents, such as the disaster that overtook the Blockley bus coming down Blockley Hill on 9th August 1924, when the brakes failed and the vehicle crashed through a stone wall, with several passengers losing their lives.

Some of the Cotswold railway bridges over lanes had been built for horse traffic, and when the bus approached it was the duty of the conductor to climb the outside stairs and call out, 'Get your heads down *if* you please,' to the top-deck passengers. Then, when everybody had complied, he would ring the bell for the bus to proceed. 'It was quite an experience,' Mr. Hearn told us, 'to duck your head and go under the bridge just as a heavy goods train was trundling overhead a few inches away, it seemed!'

Even in the 1920s there were still people in the more remote hamlets of the Cotswolds who had seldom stirred out of their cottage gardens, except to go to Church. Perhaps they would go with a party of villagers on an annual outing to far away Gloucester or

Motor bus at Chipping Norton
In times of deep snow the higher mounted balloon-tyred bus was superior to the light cars of the day, and by the early 1930s, as this scene shows, the great names in the onmibus world, including Midland Red, had established large networks serving the Midlands and the Cotswolds.

Northleach
The network of local motor bus services that grew up around the time of the First World War brought vital life to the Cotswold villages and hamlets. Many of these early buses were run by a small firm, or just one man – perhaps a garage owner. Although, as this picture shows, route numbers were already much used, the vehicles themselves were often less than reliable, and usually incapable of climbing the steeper hills with loads.

Oxford. But the daily round of work and church, and the bringing up of children filled their years. They did not know, or really care, where the trains went on the railways which crossed the countryside. Their only interest might be in a visit to the local station to meet the arrival of a relative or collect a parcel sent by relations in London. But the First World War was to change all that.

Despite the advent of the buses, one feature of the countryside was still the number of people who walked the roads and byways. There were the pedlars, who later dignified their calling with a hand-cart, then a horse and wagon, eventually calling themselves 'door-to-door salesmen' after the First World War. During that war there were increasing numbers of shabby men who seemed half-crazy – no doubt discharged from the Army with shell-shock or simply 'reported missing'. It was also a time when there were still many elderly folk living in tumbledown properties whose way of life was still very much of the Nineteenth century.

Electricity and main drainage came slowly, and although these amenities transformed the quality of life in Cirencester or Fairford, it was many years before electricity came to all the villagers off the main road, even after the pylons of the National Grid marched over the Wolds.

But even without electricity, in the 1930s villagers began to acquire wireless sets powered by batteries, and proudly displayed them amid the potted geraniums that grace every Cotswold living room window ledge. It is difficult to point out the exact time when village life became 'modern'. Perhaps one can date it approximately to when regular motor buses ran through the villages and the more wealthy ordinary villagers owned secondhand cars. The time when, perhaps, some ex-servicemen bought an Army-surplus lorry and began a transport business from the local blacksmith-come-garage. In the small towns, the first 'chain stores' arrived, their alien fronts contrasting with the sombre shops of old. One of the first was Woolworths, with plate glass windows, electric lighting and

The Red and the White
Red Bus Service outside Cheltenham College Cricket Ground about 1930. The Red Buses were to amalgamate with the White Co to form Red & White Motor Services, operating on a wide area from Newport, Monmouth to Stroud and around the Wye Valley and Forest of Dean areas. The Stroud area routes were taken over by the Bristol Omnibus Co in 1949.

centrally heated interior. The colourful signs and low prices were all so new and in contrast to the old style of shop that people from the villages went by special coach to places like Oxford, Gloucester and Stroud to see the new shops. Other chain stores were Freeman, Hardy and Willis; and Maypole, the provision and grocery merchants.

It was the arrival of chain stores that began to alter the way of rural life. At weekends families would take the new motor bus and travel much further – even into the larger towns such as Cirencester, Cheltenham and Swindon, where by the later 1930s Marks and Spencer had arrived, and there were also department stores with electric lifts. The modern store, together with the cinema, did more to change the

FATAL ACCIDENT AT LITTLE COMPTON HILL

villagers' outlook on life than ever the railways did in the 19th century.

Ideas were spread by the cinema and the wireless and the increasing numbers of visitors who came by coach and car to the area. Then, as education improved, the older children would have to travel into the towns for secondary education if they were bright. Yet, even just before 1939, there were still wayside cottages little better than hovels, and groups of ragged and dirty children staring at strangers who had driven down some lost byway to a little known hamlet. Every village still had its 'Old Charlie' who lived in a lean-to in the woods. Every hamlet had its youth with a cloth cap and vacant stare – 'the loony Dicks and Georges'. There were still some domestic servants at the big houses, but by now they were better paid, and often owned smart bicycles or motorcycles. The roads were resurfaced and long distance motor coaches and lorries thundered along trunk

routes like the A40. Tea shops opened in Burford High Street, and the crowds flocked to see the delights of Bourton-on-the-Water. Yet the railways seemed to sleep on, their remote stations seeing less traffic year by year.

The Second World War brought a last great revival of railways in the Cotswolds. New airfields and Army camps were built everywhere. Goods trains ran hour after hour and passenger trains and troop specials brought the dying lines back to life again. Towns like Fairford and Lechlade after 1943 were full of American servicemen, their jeeps and huge trucks with floppy canvas roofs roared down the rural byways, with aircraft flying night after night over the Cotswold skies.

From then on, the Cotswolds were never remote and unknown again. For a decade after 1945 Cotswold road and rail services still formed a vital part of the region's life. Then, it seemed, everybody acquired motor cars and things were changed for ever.

Terror on the highway
It was much more sensible to travel by train than road in the 1920s. Here is an accident which caused loss of life. It involved a Pickford's steam wagon and trailer from Oxford, which went out of control on Little Compton Hill resulting in a complete blockage of the road. Many telegraph wires were brought down. Steam lorries were popular at the time for moving large loads before the days of the diesel engine. They had a large fire-box from which, when it was over-stocked, bright sparks flew.

Over the Wolds and Far Away

The Pre-railway Age

In Gloucestershire
These high, wild hills and wild,
uneven ways
Draw out our miles and make
them wearisome.
(Richard II)

Centuries before Shakespeare or even the Romans, traders and travellers had been crossing the Cotswolds. Their routes can still be traced in the green trackways like the Jurassic Way (perhaps the oldest), the Ryknild, Welsh and Fosse Ways. These were the trade routes between Wales and the east, the north and the ports of the south. The routes served, too, as the ways down which invaders came and new ideas were carried. Trade was also carried out by water, using the Severn – the Portway from Roman Gloucester to the Cotswolds, is an example.

The Romans converted the Fosse Way into a military highway, running near the western edge of the Cotswolds, whilst there was Ermine Street linking Cirencester to the south and the Midlands northward. But these routes were predominately military highways. It was centuries later – the Middle Ages, when the Cotswold highways became important for the wool trade. The very name 'Coteswold' is derived from the Saxon 'cote' – a sheep fold, and 'wold' – a bare hill. Vast flocks of sheep – perhaps as many as 2,000 animals, would be driven from Wales and could take three hours or more to pass through towns like Banbury. Yet on the open wolds they could go quickly enough and it is recorded that leaving the Cotswolds on a Friday afternoon, they reached Smithfield in London, by Monday morning.

It was in those centuries after the Norman Conquest, and the gradual settling down of the area, that wool became an important industry. In fact, it became England's most important industry – which is why the Lord Chancellor even today sits on the Woolsack. Certainly, by the 14th Century it was said that 'In Europe, the best wool is English . . . in England, the best wool is Cotswold'. The sheep were sheared in the Cotswolds, the wool then being sent to the south coast to be exported to the Continent from ports such as Southampton. In fact so much of the Cotswold wool went by this route at Southampton that the merchants had a special wool staple house – which can still be seen today.

Eventually, however, trade began to move from Flanders and Lombardy to England. Flemish weavers arrived in the Cotswolds, and the great age of spinning and weaving began in towns such as Fairford, Witney, and Chipping Campden. The local merchants grew rich and soon they poured their wealth into the rebuilding of the parish churches. It is no accident that the epitaph of one merchant runs:

I praise God and ever shall
It is the sheep hath paid for all

The expanding trade increased the traffic on the roads and the need for centralised market places. Stow-on-the-Wold was a hill top town created by Henry I in 1107, when he gave the Abbot of Evesham a licence to hold a market in an area where there were no towns. Edward Stowe, as the place was originally called,

prospered into the principal sheep market of the region. Sheep fairs were held twice a year and by 1750 more than 20,000 animals passed through the market each year.

Wool spinning, and eventually cloth making, developed the wealth of the Cotswolds. Over in Witney, about 1320, one Thomas Blankett invented a type of closely woven fabric that became used for 'blankets', and they have been made there ever since.

But not only drovers and sheep filled the Cotswold highways in pre-railway times. Travellers included nobles and their vast retinues; bishops, abbots and monks; pedlars, mule trains, strolling players; robbers, and tramps. The towns along the routes provided food for men and horses, shelter and markets.

But it was always the great sheep runs and the wool industry that predominated. Cloth mills became increasingly important, harnessing power from the streams. But as the demand grew for cloth, larger mills were necessary, and eventually such upland towns as Northleach went into decline because the local streams were insufficient to drive the mills. The cloth industry moved to the Stroud area and eventually the Golden Valley became the principle industrial area. In the time of that immortal traveller and recorder, Daniel Defoe, the Stroud valley was famous for the quality of its cloth and for the dyes it used. Uley Blue and Stroud Scarlet were used for military cloth, which was increasingly in demand as the

Empire began to grow. But steam was on the way, and by the early 19th century, the mills of the Stroud valley were being converted to coal power. However the cost of transporting coal was expensive, and the industry began to lose to the better placed areas of the North. The once vast mills began to decline, and certainly among the small mills in other parts of the Cotswolds there were closures.

Other changes were in the landscape itself. As in other parts of England the former mainly open landscape of common land and scrub between the towns and villages began to be enclosed. This was a process that had begun in the 16th century, but it was increasingly put into practice by the later years of the eighteenth and early nineteenth century. The open land gave way to ditched and fenced or hedged fields, with improvements to roads. This was the time when the now famous Cotswold dry stone walls were largely created. Miles of walling were made across the open uplands, the yellow limestone standing up against the browns and greens of the landscape. But this newness did not appeal to all travellers. Naturally, that grumbling economist and traveller, William Cobbett had his say: 'Anything so ugly I have never seen in my life.' But the years of weather have mellowed the walls, and today they are admired for the skill of their construction and their satisfying appearance.

The Enclosures created new roads as well. For instance, the Oxford to Cheltenham highway was straightened out, and some of the towns on its formerly torturous route were by-passed – Burford for example. Stage coach services were improved and a service of turnpike trusts was established by 1760, with toll houses where money was paid by all who passed, for the upkeep of the improved roads. Inns were enlarged, and better services provided for swift changes of horses, so that travel became quicker. By 1815 the Cotswold main roads were the routes of such stage coach services as The

Defiant; *The Rival, The Dart* and *The Regulator* – each with its well-known driver. These were mighty men indeed. Their ruddy faces and a wide girth marked them out amongst men. They wore massive and multi-coloured overcoats and scarves against the bitter winds. Their driving and their linguistic skills were renowned – hence Dickens' celebrated descriptions. Drivers like Black Will; Cheesman and Charles Horn knew how to handle a mail coach even in the worst of winter storms, and to get the best out of their teams of horses as they battled their way over the high hills. But the ordinary Cotswold folk only watched these fast moving vehicles rattle past. Their lives were bound by custom and the few miles around the nearest market town. London was almost a legendary place and even Oxford, Gloucester or Bristol, were places that many visited only once in a lifetime.

The transportation of goods was still a slow and expensive process, despite the improved roads of the eighteenth century. It was the carrier who was responsible for transporting the majority of things. Some of the vehicles travelled as far as London, and were fed by local carrier services, which ran through the villages and hamlets tucked away in the valleys and hollows.

Main carriers, such as the Banbury to London service, were pulled by teams of eight horses. The wagon had special broad wheels to navigate the ruts and holes of the roads. Slung under the floor of the cart was a kind of gondolier carrying pigs and chickens, as well as food for these animals, and the horses. The heaviest goods were packed on the floor of the wagon and the load was gradually and skilfully built up so that the lightest items were up by the canvas roof. The front and rear of the cart were protected by heavy water-proofed curtains. At night, horn lanterns cast a low light as the load rumbled along its regular course. The drivers, like the stage coach men, had to be strong and healthy.

They performed a vital task in an age when there were no other means of communication between places except by horseback or walking. Yet they enjoyed their life and privileged position in rural society. They were the people who saw other regions and met a wide range of men. There was an old Cotswold song that ran:

My name is Jim, the carter lad,
A jolly cock am I,
I always am contented
Be the weather wet or dry,
I snap my fingers at the snow,
And whistle at the rain,
I've braved the storm for many a
day
And can do so again.

By the end of Georgian times canals were being constructed in many parts of the country. It was natural that the merchants of the Stroud Valley should turn their attention to these revolutionary ways of transporting goods – particularly as a means of obtaining coal supplies. In fact, they were some of the earliest merchants to consider transport by canal. As early as 1697 there had been proposals for a waterway, but this met with years of opposition from others, who argued that the water level of the river would be reduced and the mills would suffer. In the following century Acts of Parliament were granted for the building of waterways to link the Severn with Stroud (1730 to 1779). The proposed waterway would run under Cirencester Park and it was the poet Alexander Pope, a frequent visitor there, who predicted that the waters of the Thames and Severn would be joined. In 1722 he wrote to a friend: 'the meeting of the Thames and Severn which . . . are to be led into each other's embraces thro' secret caverns of not above twelve or fifteen miles, till they rise and openly celebrate their marriage in the midst of an immense amphitheatre, which is to be the admiration of posterity a hundred years hence.' The 'immense amphitheatre' did not materialise, but the tunnel did – beneath the trees and grasslands of the park.

Birdlip Hill – A scene of about 1938
Birdlip Hill rises some 700ft above the Severn Plain at Gloucester up to the Cotswold Edge. Despite improvements, many B roads were still full of dangerous bends, but there was really very little traffic except at weekends. The car at the side of the road seems to have failed to climb the hill and has been left rather dangerously parked.

The bicycling craze

A cycling party about to set out on a country tour after arriving at a local station, probably Chipping Norton, in July 1904. As Betjeman wrote:

'With a one-inch map
A bicycle and well-worn "Little Guide"
Those were the years I used to Ride for miles to far-off churches'

For lady cyclists, as with lady motorists, the new modes of transport were fraught with difficulty because of the dangers of catching their long coats in the rear wheels. The problem was overcome by Mrs Bloomer and the special cycling outfits. Later rear mudguards were strung to keep clothes from the rear spokes.

The cycle gave a new sense of freedom, and in the brief period when lanes were metalled but not tarred, and the motor car was not yet a threat, the cyclist tackled quite long distances. In this picture nobody seems to bother about lamps, although a gas burner was soon on the market, giving a fierce and brilliant light.

The young were told to regard cycling as an adventure. In the '*Boys' Own Paper*' 1906, an article suggests that readers repeat the excitement of a ride from London during the hours of darkness:

'Darkness gives an involuntary thrill. Eyes wander to the ground to see the dimly luminous circle cast by the lamp. You are not quite sure where the road is. You know it is *somewhere* beneath you, but you are not sure on which side you are riding.'

35

Then, in 1781, a meeting was held at the King's Head Hotel in Cirencester to set up a committee and start a subscription list for the building of a canal to link Stroud with the Thames. The route was surveyed by Robert Whitworth, who is said to have been assisted by Thomas Brindley, the canal pioneer.

In 1783 work began on the Thames and Severn Canal and the first section from Stroud to Chalford was completed in 1785. But the difficult part of the scheme was the section from near Chalford, south to the Thames at Lechlade. The work was to involve the boring of the longest canal tunnel in England (and what was to be the third longest tunnel in the world at that period). It was to be reached by a series of locks and was two miles long. The work took five years – a remarkably quick time for such a job at that date. At the south end the tunnel entrance was a classical archway with niches in which it was intended to place statues of Father Thames, and Sabrina, the

goddess of the Severn. On 19th July 1788, King George III paid a visit to see the advanced state of the work there.

At Lechlade, the Thames was now navigable for barges of up to 70 tons down to Oxford, and then to London.

The tunnel opened in April 1789, and the craft were moved through it by 'legging'. The crew lay on wooden planks across the boat and literally 'walked' the walls, a procedure that took three hours, the only light being from a guttering lantern. The tunnel had a passing place in the centre, but it must have been a frightening journey – especially in the cold and damp of the Gloucestershire winter. The horses were meanwhile led over the hills above by teams of local boys, who earned their livelihood this way. But it was not unknown for an empty boat to take the horses along with it.

Despite the engineering triumphs, the tunnel and canal were always very difficult to maintain. Almost from the start

there was trouble with the water levels. The canal had a fairly short life because the building of the Great Western Railway through the valley in 1845 seriously affected its prosperity. The canal's receipts dropped from £11,000 in

Problem on the road
A Wolseley saloon fills up in a lane near Chipping Norton in March 1939. Large petrol stations did not exist during the first decades of motoring, and a major problem was always where to find petrol, when on a lengthy trip. Most cars carried spare cans of petrol, but service in many cases from the casually-sited filling points was indifferent and unreliable. The pumps were only manned if the proprietor happened to be around at the time. At this site petrol appears to be drawn from open-sited barrels, which must have been a great fire risk. The fluid was hand-cranked to the upper vessels, so that the motorist could see the spirit in the glass containers. It then went by gravity down the pipe to the tank of the car. In this case the petrol is Shell. Note the enamelled iron pump sign in the shape of a shell. Garages did not keep exclusively to one type of petrol and often a whole range would be available – a system that did not die out until after the Second World War. When the signs were discarded, they were often used to repair sheds beside the garage.

36

1841 to £3,000 in 1855. By 1865 there were plans to turn part of the canal route into a road. The GWR purchased the section from Lechlade to Chalford, including the tunnel, but subsequently the canal was administered by a Trust, consisting of representatives of local councils and canal companies. The Trust set about restoration and by 1895 navigation was restored, but the problems with water leakage caused a further abandonment in 1901. The Gloucestershire County Council then took up responsibility and there was a further restoration scheme from 1901 to 1907. The canal declined over the next few years and on 11 May 1911, the last commercial boat passed through the tunnel, carrying a load of stone. Abandonment of the canal came after the First World War – Whitehall Bridge to Lechlade, in the summer of 1927, and the remainder above Stroud from June 1933.

The final years of the canal's working life are described in that classic book *The Flower of Gloster* by E. Temple Thurston. He came along the Golden Valley in 1911 and on the way met a canal character, 'Old William' who was a lengthman. William's job was to keep the hedges trimmed and the vegetation from overhanging the navigation. William spent much of his time waiting for boats that never came. He told Thurston that he was reluctant to let the Canal Company know how few boats used his length of the 'cut'. 'I don't know what they as be going to do about this canal – there gets less water in her every day.'

Slowly moving up the Golden Valley, Thurston records that:
the grey houses, with their blue slate roofs, grew fewer in number, the hills at each side become higher; there are broader pasture fields; a stray farm or a lock house is all you can see of human habitation. In the nearer distance, the dense woods spread over the rolling landscape, like an army in glittering mail, with golden trappings and columned plumes, they march down the hillsides to the water's edge.

Already the canal traffic was in steep decline, despite the efforts by the County Council to improve the locks and navigation.

The whole way from Stroud upwards is almost deserted now. We only met one barge in the whole journey. An old lady with a capacious bonnet was standing humming quietly to herself at the tiller. That was the only barge we found on those waters.

The *Flower of Gloster* was coaxed into the stygian gloom of the Sapperton Tunnel. Somehow, canal tunnels have so much more of a frightening aspect than railway tunnels. Perhaps the steam and soot of a railway tunnel makes it more friendly! 'Into the grim darkness you glide

Northleach
If you look on the right carefully you can see the photographer's motor cycle combination. Mr Packer used this machine until the late '30s. The Unicorn Hotel was a well known stop for travellers and next door, J. A. Hill's Cycle & Motor Agent did a good trade with passing travellers.

Sowing the seed
Life on the open fields could be hard indeed for men such as this. Here an ancient seed sowing device is still in use in Oxfordshire about 1900.

Poachers
This photograph, though posed, bears some marks of truth. Seldom would poachers be as encumbered as this. Gamekeepers were extremely active and the art of poaching called for good ears, a sense of smell and keen eyesight.

Spring guns were set during Victorian times, designed to kill and maim, just as the poacher set traps and slings for his animal and bird victims. The occasional poached rabbit or fowl was regarded by many as an essential part of a family's survival during times of economic depression.

and within half an hour are lost in a lightless cavern where the drip of the clammy water sounds increasingly in your ears,' wrote Thurston. Apparently, professional 'leggers' had been employed to move the craft through the tunnel, but by his time the practice had ceased. The author and his companion had to 'leg' for themselves. 'It was evening when we came out into the light again and, although the sun had set, with shadows falling everywhere, it almost dazzled me.'

Although the commercial traffic through the tunnel had ceased, pleasure craft occasionally made the trip. One of the very last boats of all was in 1912, when the ladies and gentlemen of the Brimscombe Polytechnic College made the rather frightening trip – unsuitable for sufferers from claustrophobia. By 1916, falls from the roof made the passage impassable.

The other Cotswold area canal was the Oxford. This waterway was a continuation of the Birmingham to Banbury Canal of 1778. The Oxford section was opened in 1790 and the construction was under the supervision of James Brindley, the 'father of canals', the work being completed after his death by Robert Whitwell and Samuel Simock. At Oxford, the canal linked with the Thames. Not only was cargo carried, but there was a service of passenger 'fly boats'. Drawn by teams of horses, they offered a slower, but smoother ride than the stage coaches. But they were no serious competition because of the time spent negotiating the very numerous series of locks north of Banbury. Trade on the Oxford Canal lasted until as recently as 1961. The connection at Oxford with the Thames was filled in, and Nuffield College stands on the site. But the wharves near the city centre were converted into a base for the now very popular canal holidays. The Oxford Canal is one of the most busy routes for inland waterway holidays.

Waiting for the bus
The well dressed man on the left is carefully guarding some bulky cases and was almost certainly a commercial traveller; no company cars or titles like 'sales representative' then. The scene dates from the early 1920s and was taken near Little Barrington.

Sapperton Tunnel – 1903
The Gothic-style west portal at the head of the Stroud valley. The hamlet of Daneway here began as a settlement for the labourers who built the tunnel. It was also the terminus of the canal until the tunnel southwards was completed in 1789. The cottages were for the canal 'Lengthmen', who maintained the tow path and kept a watch on the state of the canal banks. They also kept the undergrowth down along the canal side. The nearby Bricklayers Arms pub was originally built by John Nock in 1784 as a hostel. With the wharf, it was a convenient stopping place on the canal journey, where exhausted men who had legged the tunnel from Sapperton could relax, or, alternatively fortify themselves for the three hour voyage through the damp and dark.

Sapperton Tunnel
The south entrance after the modern restoration. The empty niches were intended for statues of the Goddess of the Severn, Sabrina, and Isis, Goddess of the Thames. The crown of the tunnel was 250ft below the surface of the hills. The tunnel was 15ft 4ins wide and the roof 10ft 4ins above the water. The first boat passed through on 20 April 1789, although the canal was not fully operational until 19 November of that year.

Near Ebley
A scene from the days when horses plodded their way along the lower part of the Thames-Severn Canal even in the 1920s, long after closure of the upper reaches of the waterway.

The Burford Bus – 1889
Some passengers were able to sit beside the driver, whilst the tiny and cramped saloon must have been very stuffy indeed.

Donkey transport
The steep tracks up to the settlements on the sides of the Golden Valley at Stroud were unsuitable for wheeled transport. So donkeys were used, and they were even fitted with metal panniers to carry coal. This old picture shows as pair of coal donkeys in the lane at Streates Hill at the turn of the century.

Heavy goods vehicle
Typical Cotswold wagon used for the
transport of goods to and from the rural
stations. This vehicle was based at
Notgrove on the Banbury-Cheltenham
line.

Milton-under-Wychwood (Oxfordshire)
The ancient forest of Wychwood was
noted for the quality of its oaks, many of
which went to build the ships of England's
navy. The forest had largely been cleared
by the early 19th century. But Wychwood
timber was still in demand as late as the
early 1930s, when this picture was taken.

Intrepid travellers through the Sapperton Tunnel
Despite a journey of 2 miles that took 3 hours, propelling the barge by legging along the walls, there were several pleasure outings through the damp stygian darkness. This party consists of stalwart members of the Brimscombe Polytechnic in 1912.

Swindon to Gloucester

We have already mentioned the GWR line from Swindon to Gloucester. But this was not the first railway connected with the Cotswold area. A horse drawn railway was opened from Moreton-in-Marsh to Shipston-on-Stour in 1826. Its opening was an event of great celebration and there was even a song sung in taverns and at harvest homes for many years afterwards about the technological wonder:

> Good people all of Moreton
> Town
> Give ear to what I say,
> We all have reason to rejoice
> On this our market day.
> To see our iron railway
> It makes one's heart content
> To know what's saved in firing
> Will nearly pay our rent.

The 'tramway' was profitable, unlike the canals, and in its early years, made an annual profit of about £3,000. Eventually the line was rented by the Oxford, Worcester & Wolverhampton Railway. A twice daily passenger service (still horse drawn) was run from 1853 connecting Moreton to Stratford. The line was last used about 1904, although not legally abandoned until 1926.

To return to the Stroud Valley and the Gloucester line. In 1836, the people of Cheltenham obtained an Act for a 'Cheltenham & Great Western Union Railway'. One of the routes was to be via Birmingham and the South Midlands to the Vale of Aylesbury. Trains would have been hauled up the Cotswold Edge at Cheltenham. The plan prompted the Great Western to appoint Brunel to survey a line from Swindon to Stroud and Gloucester. He made a thorough survey of what was a difficult terrain and proposed a line having a ruling gradient of 1 in 330, with a tunnel 2,830 yards long at Sapperton. Work on the line began and at Sapperton a number of exploratory shafts were sunk in 1841, on behalf of the Cheltenham Company. But because of financial difficulties, the project was taken over by the GWR and resumed in August 1841. A fresh survey was then made and the tunnel subsequently constructed at a higher level, the tunnel being 2,730 yards long. The contractor was Jonathan Nowell of Wickwar. The work was completed in a remarkably short time for that age, and the first passenger trains ran through the tunnel on Whit Monday, 12 May 1845. The final section from the junction with the Midland Railway at Standish was opened in May and trains ran through to Cheltenham via Gloucester on 23 October 1847. Because of the nature of the landscape, the line had a great many bridges and short viaducts, some built of wood (replacements in brick and iron were completed in 1859).

Just south of Kemble station, the line passed through a short 'cut-and-cover' tunnel to comply with wishes of the local landowners, the Gordon family. The Gordons were very strict about the railway and were able to extract a number of conditions from the GWR, including the promise that no drink would be sold at the station, or a public house built nearby. This state of affairs lasted until the railways were nationalised in 1948.

As well as the line to Cirencester, Kemble was also the junction for the Tetbury branch from 1889, of which more later. It was during the building of the original station at Kemble that a spring of pure water was tapped and it was connected to a pipe which filled water tenders for conveyance down the line to the Swindon works. In 1903 a pipe was laid alongside the railway to Swindon. The line to Stroud and Gloucester was also the main line to South Wales before the building of the Severn Tunnel. The heavy trains, particularly of coal, would be assisted up the gradients from the Stroud Valley to Sapperton by banking locomotives kept at Brimscombe – the 'Brimscombe Bankers'.

The town of Tetbury in the south west Costwolds lies in the heart of the hunting and horse country. It was a place that even William Cobbett found 'a very pretty town' when he passed that way in 1826. The line from Kemble to Tetbury opened on 2 December 1899, various intermediate stations being added later. The first stop from Kemble was Rodmarton Platform, opened in 1904. Apparently the term 'platform' was borrowed from the Scottish railways and denoted that the 'station' had a full length platform (in contrast to a halt), with simple accommodation for an assistant porter, who could issue tickets and book luggage. A 'halte' later spelt without the 'e', was simply a stopping place.

Culkerton Station had a

Kemble

A busy scene about 1905, with 'up' train for Swindon. The track to the right is the Cirencester branch, and the vehicles to the extreme right contain gas cylinders used for carriage lighting. These cylinders were recharged at Swindon.

Kemble station was built in 1872 on this site (previously it had been situated a little north towards the Cotswolds). The Tetbury branch started from the left hand platform, beyond the station buildings.

Kemble

Looking north with the Tetbury branch platform and track to the left, behind the water tower.

moderately-sized goods shed. The station closed in 1956, only to have a short new lease of life in 1959, when the branch was provided with a diesel rail car service. Another station was at Jackaments Bridge Halt, opened in 1939 to serve the nearby RAF base (it was closed in 1948). A halt was opened as late as 1956 at the quaintly named Trouble House. It served a nearby pub of that name; the title is said to have originated from the days when agricultural workers rioted against the introduction of machinery.

In its early days the Tetbury line was busy with much horse-box traffic, particularly to the Duke of Beaufort's estate. Many famous people travelled by train to Tetbury to take part in weekend polo and hunting activities. In fact, so heavy was this traffic, that the original terminus buildings were rebuilt in 1913. There was a single locomotive shed and the branch engine was kept there overnight. There is a story that sometimes the station staff arrived late in the morning and had difficulty in getting the locomotive's steam up ready for the first train.

Tetbury lies in lush country and nearby is the world famous Westonbirt Arboretum founded in 1820 by Robert Holford. Westonbirt House is now an exclusive school for girls.

To return to the Stroud line and its subsequent history; by the early 1900s, the Great Western was already forseeing competition from road vehicles, perhaps far in advance of the other railways at the time. At the Company's Half Yearly Meeting in August 1903, Lord Cawdor, the Chairman, announced to his surprised shareholders:

> We are putting on a motor car service, a combined car which will carry about 52 passengers. We can run trains over the line, stopping not only at stations, but with the sanction of the Board of Trade, at lane crossings, and at roads coming up to the line.

The 'motor car' he referred to was a special saloon carriage designed by G. J. Churchward. It incorporated a steam engine unit mounted on a bogie. The vehicle had a top speed of 45mph.

The new service along the Stroud valley began on 12 October 1903, between Stonehouse and Chalford. The saloon was fitted with retractable steps which enabled passengers to be set down or picked up at places where there were no platforms. A number of short 'haltes' (a Belgium railway term) were opened along the line. The novelty of this new type of train attracted crowds of passengers and by the end of the year there was an increase of 8% in traffic.

'I believe there is a considerable future for motor cars on rails,' said Lord Cawdor. The result of this initial success was that no less than 44 further vehicles were ordered for the GWR system, some being trailers. By the end of 1903, some 2,500 passengers per week were being carried on the Stroud valley service and the trains were subsequently extended to Gloucester. By 1914, Stroud station had to be rebuilt to deal with the crowds, many coming to sample the then growing shopping centre. By that time the 'motor cars' and their trailer carriages were a familiar part of the Great Western scene.

Kemble
A scene from the late 1950s, with a southbound train.

In the 1920s further batches of saloons were built, the steam motor bogies gradually being phased out and the original vehicles adapted for running with permanently coupled 0-6-0 tank locomotives. Apparently the heat and dirt of the old steam bogies incorporated in the saloons was unpleasant, particularly in the summer, and proved unpopular with passengers and crews. Stroud had another station on the Midland Railway, it was an extension of the line from Nailsworth and Stonehouse. The Stonehouse railway dated from 1867, its purpose being to bring coal to the mills in the lower part of the Stroud valley. It was originally an independent concern, but became associated with the Midland Railway in 1878 and was purchased outright in 1888. The short extension to Stroud from Stonehouse opened in 1885. The Stroud terminus was linked by a covered footpath to the GWR station.

The Great Western line through the Stroud valley continued to carry heavy traffic even after the Severn Tunnel was opened. It was the inter-war years, however, which saw a great speeding up of passenger train services to Cheltenham, culminating in the famous Cheltenham Flyer. Introduced on 9 July 1923, it was acclaimed by 1929 as the world's fastest train, with a record run on 6 June 1932 to Paddington with an average speed of 71.4mph. The popular auto train services that had originated as the Edwardian 'rail motors' continued to operate until 1958, when diesel multiple unit trains took over the stopping services between Swindon and Gloucester, with a number of stations south of the Sapperton tunnel being closed.

Cirencester
The trees and wall in the background mark the boundary of Lord Bathurst's estate – Cirencester Park. After the closure of the branch from Kemble in 1964, the forecourt of the Cirencester terminus became a bus station, although this is now little used.

Cirencester
Jackson's ironmongery shop (left) and
Cricklade Street about 1903.

Cirencester about 1912/13
A consignment of tractors just delivered
from the makers. The works numbers
appear to be drawn on the fuel tanks. The
tractors are about to be driven to the
agricultural machinery showrooms of
W. G. Bridges.

*A Consignment of Titan Tractors for
W. G. Bridges, Cirencester*

Steam rolling
Keeping the roads rolled was important in the days before many were tarmac surfaced. This Fowler steam roller was photographed in Edwardian days near Aldsworth on the road from Burford to Bibury. One of the men is standing with oil can in hand ready to lubricate the machinery. But surely the two children have been posed in their Sunday best clothes?

Steam lorries
A familiar sight on Cotswold roads. This Sentinel has just arrived from the manufacturer's plant in Shrewsbury and still carries trade plates.

Kemble
A mixed train waiting in the sidings at Kemble. The brake van is lettered 'Tetbury'. The auto train was used for services for many years.

Rodmarton

This is a typical Great Western 'platform'. The distinction compared with a 'halt' was that a 'platform' was longer and usually had a resident attendant and a small hut where he could sell tickets and handle goods. Apparently the term came from Scottish Railways.

Culkerton

Like the other stops on the line, it had become rather run down by the time the line was closed in 1964. It used to have a goods shed building, which still existed when the authors came along this way in the early 1980s.

Culkerton

A photograph after the first closure in 1954. With the introduction of the four-wheel diesel railbus in 1959 it was re-opened and for a few years traffic was good. In fact, two other halts were opened. One was at Trouble House, said to be the only station in Britain serving a pub! The name is said to have come from the early nineteenth century agrarian riots in the area. Another halt was opened in 1955 at Church Hill.

Tetbury

The station was rebuilt in 1913 to cater for the busy traffic in visitors and their horses. For this is hunting and jumping countryside. There was a small engine shed and it was the daily duty of the station staff to get the locomotive ready. Sometimes they were late and the first train suffered. But even though this was 'God's Wonderful Railway' where discipline reigned, there were many blind eyes turned to the more rural parts of the system.

Tetbury

The years have moved on to the 1960s. The old station looks a little forlorn and the once busy tracks were only used by the four-wheeler diesel car from Kemble and the rare goods train.

Sapperton Tunnel

This was 1864 yards long and was divided by a short open section which provided a welcome relief for the steam locomotive crews after the long and smokey climb through the darkness.

Sapperton (*top left*)
Climbing up through the wooded valley is a 2800 Class locomotive, No. 2875 with a freight train from the South West (via Gloucester) in June 1962.

Chalford (*bottom left*)
Auto train photographed on 9 June 1964, shortly before local services were withdrawn. The locomotive is a '1400' Class 0-4-2T, No. 1451, built in 1935 and used until the 1950s in the Exeter area. The locomotive was scrapped in July 1964.

Chalford (*top right*)
Steam rail motor No. 2 pauses at the platform before setting out on its journey down the valley to Stroud and Gloucester. This pioneer vehicle was of the S type and was 70ft long. It was rebuilt in 1918.

Chalford (*centre*)
The hilly surroundings can be seen here. Many of the larger buildings are former cloth mills dating back to the seventeenth century. The canal brought coal for their operation by the end of the eighteenth century, and later, the railway performed this role.

Chalford (*bottom right*)
A two car auto train about 60 years ago.

Chalford Station

Chalford, The Golden Valley.

Chalford

A fine view of the Golden Valley. The young boy at the bottom right hand corner in his sailor suit dates this picture to before 1914. The GWR line can be seen high up on the left.

Chalford

Busy times in pre-1914 days. A local train for Swindon is just leaving, whilst one of the steam rail cars is in the bay platform. In the goods yard a carrier's wagon drawn by two hefty horses is loading up. The tow-path beside the silent Thames-Severn Canal is clearly seen behind the trains.

Chalford
The high ground just behind the 'down' platform was a popular place for photographers over the years. Notice how the groups of houses cover the hillside, reached by lanes so steep and narrow that they were all but impassable to early motors.

Pioneer steam rail car at Chalford
The thickly populated Stroud Valley provided plenty of traffic for the GWR local trains, particularly after 1903 when the first steam railcars were introduced.

The additional glass window lights above the driver's window were inserted after drivers complained that they could not see properly.

Chalford
A scene from the early 1960s with an auto train simmering in the siding to the right. Trains terminated here on the Gloucester local service.

Brimscombe
The Broad Gauge had just been lifted and standard width track installed on the old base when this view of Brimscombe was taken – probably at the completion of the work.

Brimscombe
The Victoria Hotel was the base for 'A. Eddels Omnibus Proprietor Wedding carriages, wagonettes for hire'. The gentlemen on this vehicle are looking forward to a trip to the Cotswolds.

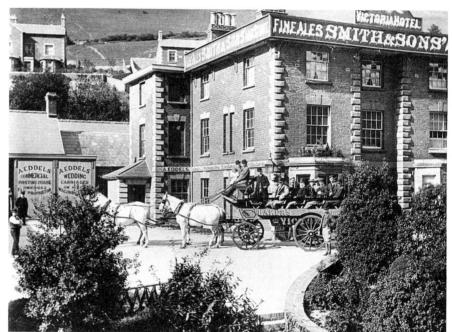

Brimscombe
A southbound express in the 1950s.

Brimscombe
A freight train awaits assistance in the distant loop line ready for the steep haul up to the Sapperton tunnel.

Stroud
Swindon bound train of clerestory stock approaching Capels Mill Viaduct about 1900. The vehicles in the Stroud yard on the right are of the type known as 'iron minks'.

Early motor bus
The Cheltenham-Painswick-Stroud service near Stroud. The route began as far as Painswick in 1902.

Stroud
Early GWR bus standing outside the south side of the station. Apparently the group of people includes the station staff and perhaps their families, as well as at least one of the steam rail motor crews from the railway.

Off to the match
Charabanc believed to be carrying supporters and players of the Chalford Football team photographed at Horseponds Hill, Brookthorpe on the way from Chalford to Gloucester. The driver was Mr Hopkins.

Chevrolet bus
Standish Lane terminus, Stonehouse 1930. The vehicle is one run by the Red Bus Service and was a six-wheeled model. The rear wheels were all driven but only one set actually had brakes, so stopping could be a problem on some of the steeper hills. The driver seen here on the left is E. Wilkins.

Leyland Tiger
Saloon coach of the Red Bus Co about to leave the George Street offices at Stroud for London in 1931. The time is nearly 3 pm, and the passengers will be in London at 7 pm. Note the kangaroo emblem on the bus to the right of Inspector Grimmett. It was the trade sign of Australian born Dick Reyne, owner of the firm.

Nailsworth
One time the headquarters of the old Stonehouse & Nailsworth Railway Company. The original length of line connecting the Midland main line (at Standish) to Nailsworth was opened in September 1867. Always in severe financial difficulties, it was eventually vested in the Midland Railway from 1878, and the company dissolved in 1886.

Nailsworth
In Victorian days the area was popular with tourists from far afield who came to see the village of Amberley, said to have been the 'Enderley' of Mrs Craig's *John Halifax, Gentleman*. The train seen here is hauled by one of Kirtley's outside frame engines.

Stroud's other station in September 1910
The Midland Railway terminus was at the end of the short branch from Dudbridge Junction, on the Nailsworth Line, built by the Midland in 1886. The line carried up to 3,000 tons of coal to Stroud Gas Works as late as 1970, when the line was finally closed. This was one of a number of pictures of the Stroud area taken by Gerald Drummond, a young man who was later killed in France in 1917, his last photograph dating from July of that year.

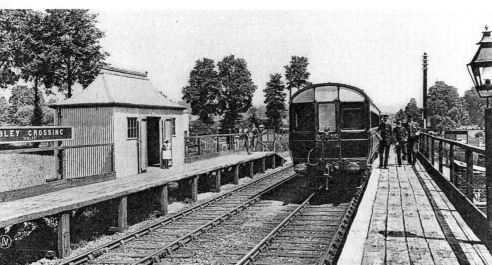

Ebley Crossing Halt
The train here is No. 50 of the auto-cars (B type of 1907). It was a 70 ft long vehicle. The delightful pagoda style waiting hut was a familiar sight at Great Western Halts. Ebley was one of a number of similar stopping places introduced for the Stroud Valley rail motor services in 1903.

St Mary's Crossing
Class 1400 No. 1453 puffing up the gradient to Stroud in June 1964, a few weeks before withdrawal of local train services.

Oxford to Banbury

For centuries, Banbury has been the most important town in the far north of Oxfordshire, just a few miles from the Cotswolds. The town had been a centre for the wool trade, as well as a staging post for travellers, coaches and flocks of animals. The manufacture of special cloths was also carried on in the villages around the town, the speciality being 'plush', that material so loved of Victorian carriage upholsterers. The Banbury region, incorporating parts of Northamptonshire and Warwickshire, had such a distinct identity that it became known as 'Banburyshire' at one period.

As early as 1848, Bernard Samuels and Joseph Gardiner established a factory for making farm machinery at Banbury. Their business grew to become world famous. Banbury Cattle Market was said to be the largest in Europe and is still very important today. Although Banbury was linked to the Midlands and Oxford by the Oxford Canal, the coming of the Great Western Railway from Oxford in 1852 put the town on the railway map.

The line started life as 'The Oxford & Rugby Railway', a project of 1844 supported by the GWR. It was to have been a Broad Gauge line, but was vetoed by a Board of Trade Committee. However, the Oxford & Rugby Railway Bill was passed by Parliament. The line was to link at Fenny Compton, north of Banbury with another projected line from Birmingham. This was the age of the 'Gauge War' between the standard gauge (today's 4ft 8½inch) and Brunel's Broad Gauge of 7ft. Eventually, the GWR went to Court over the gauge to be used on the Oxford to Fenny Compton (via Banbury) line and won its case. Work began on the line in 1846, but lack of sound finance resulted in slow progress and the Oxford & Rugby Company was taken over by the GWR. The railway was then built as a single track Broad Gauge line from Oxford to Banbury. Another two years were to pass before the railway was extended from Banbury to Fenny Compton, and at the same time, the Oxford-Banbury line was doubled, and converted to 'mixed gauge'. The public opening between Banbury and Birmingham was in 1852.

A special train hauled by the celebrated GWR locomotive *Lord of the Isles*, trundled along through the Oxfordshire countryside passing Tackley and Lower Heyford, packed with dignitaries, including the famous Locomotive Superintendant, Daniel Gooch. They were all looking forward to the customary 'cold collation' and plenty of good wine at Birmingham. Then disaster struck! As the train approached Aynho, it passed a disused signal which should have been removed when the line was widened. It was in the 'off' position and *Lord of the Isles* travelled majestically along to catch up with the tail end of a goods train in front. The driver of this goods train fortunately had the presence of mind to start his train, thus averting what could have been a major disaster. But even so, *Lord of the Isles* struck the rear wagons, smashing them to pieces and suffering the indignity of bending its own buffer beam. The guests were thrown about, but fortunately nobody was seriously hurt. It was rather mixed publicity for the new line! But it did emphasise the stability of the Broad Gauge, in that the special train was not pushed off the track. Eventually another engine came up and took the dusty and shaken guests on to Birmingham and a late meal.

The main line to Banbury leaves Oxford alongside the Canal, and in steam days the stations were at Kidlington (for Woodstock), Bletchington, Heyford, Fritwell and Somerton, Aynho, King's Sutton, where it was joined by the Princes Risborough-Bicester-Banbury main line, and also the Banbury-Cheltenham Line.

At Kidlington, the branch line ran over the fairly flat, yet pleasing landscape to Woodstock. It was in the 18th century at Woodstock that Blenheim Palace was built as the nation's gift to the Duke of Marlborough for his European victories. The magnificent palace – sometimes called the 'Versailles of England' – dominates the small town, situated on the main road from Oxford to Stratford, and for many years a centre of the glove making trade.

The elaborate social life of the Marlboroughs naturally brought the famous figures of history to Woodstock. But it is surprising that there was no railway station here until quite late in the 19th century. In 1890, the Woodstock Railway Company was formed, the Duke of Marlborough being the principal shareholder. The short line was opened to passenger trains on 19 May 1890, goods traffic being handled later. The terminus at Woodstock was opposite the gates of Blenheim, so that the Duke and his guests could be met at the station and conveyed into the park. The GWR worked the trains, subsequently acquiring the Woodstock Company in 1897 for £15,000. The trains, which sometimes included the Duke's special saloon, were worked by a 2-4-2 tank engine number 4773 *Fair Rosamund*. Over the years this tiny engine became a famous feature of the line until she was finally withdrawn in 1935. She was named after Henry VIII's mistress who lived in what was then Old Woodstock Manor at Blenheim. The locomotive used

to be kept in a shed at Woodstock until 1927, then at the Oxford Depot. The line was an early post-war closure, the last passenger train running in 1954.

A serious accident happened on Christmas Eve 1874 at Shipton. The ex-London train running behind an Armstrong 7ft single (No. 478) was already full when it reached Oxford, so it was augmented by the attachment of an ancient four-wheeled carriage, as well as a second locomotive. As the now very heavy train rattled towards Banbury on its long journey to Birkenhead, the 14 carriage train had just left Kidlington (then called Woodstock Road) at about 4mph. Not long before the train was to cross a bridge over the river Cherwell at Shipton, one of the wheels of the ancient four-wheel carriage broke up. An alarm having been raised,

the crew of the leading locomotive put on their brakes too suddenly, causing the rest of the train to crunch the damaged carriage to pieces, so that most of the train then derailed and fell into the river at Shipton Bridge. The result was that 34 passengers were killed and 65 injured. The rear guard and two passengers ran back to Woodstock Road to stop the next train, whilst the southbound train was stopped further up the line towards Aynho.

Oxford
Interior of the L&NWR terminus before the First World War. A Webb 2-4-2 simmers on the right-hand side waiting for the journey across the Oxfordshire fields to the Vale of Aylesbury and Verney Junction, where one could change to the Metropolitan Railway.

Oxford

On 1 December 1881, horse trams began in Oxford and 992 people availed themselves of this advanced form of urban transport. Eventually, routes linked the GWR station to Cowley Road High Street and Magdalen bridge. The average speed was 8 mph – roughly about the same as a motor bus of today in the rush hour. But there were never any electric trams. The University and the City felt that the overhead wires would be unsightly. No doubt, they were right. The last horse tram ran in 1913, and the services were then superseded by an extensive network of motor buses, including 34 seater Daimlers, seen here at the Cowley Road terminus.

Oxford

Over the hills and far away . . . there's an eager crowd of passengers anxious to sample this new wonder of the transport age outside the GWR station. Introduced on 29 October 1928, the GWR 'road conveyance' service provided a speedy and useful link between Oxford and Cheltenham along the A40, with pick-up points at Witney, Burford and Northleach.

The smart Thorneycroft was comfortable to ride in but one can image the rigours of a Cotswold winter, with the draughts and rain that surely must have eventually found their way under the canvas roof. The service ran four times a day and was later run by the Bristol Omnibus Company. The single fair was 12 shillings all the way from Paddington by train to Oxford. By coach the fare was only 4 shillings.

Kidlington

This station was called Woodstock Road until 19 May 1890, when the Woodstock branch opened. If you look at the right-hand side you can see *Fair Rosamund* waiting to haul the Woodstock branch train. A main line express with clerestory carriages is standing at the northbound (Banbury) platform.

Woodstock

For much of its life the branch was worked by locomotive No. 1473, *Fair Rosamund*. She was the only named tank locomotive ever owned by the GWR and until 1927 was based in a shed at Woodstock. She was withdrawn in 1935 and a report in the *Railway Magazine* of that year described her steaming north through alien country to the breakers yard. The strange thing about this picture is that it was taken at Chipping Norton. It is not known why but perhaps she was used on a special train: the crew are all posed as if this is a notable occasion.

Woodstock

The Ducal terminus with the branch train in charge of '*Fair Rosamund*'. Woodstock won the GWR London Division prizes year after year for its flowers and gardens.

Woodstock

The Woodstock branch locomotive, Class 517 *Fair Rosamund*, waits with her auto carriage at Oxford not long before she was withdrawn from service in 1935. She worked the Woodstock branch from its opening in 1890.

Woodstock

The town centre in the early 1930s, when it did not seem to matter where you parked the car – or even the bus! The strange looking lattice tower on the right carries wires for the local electricity supply.

Bletchington

Typical rural station on the OW&WR.

Heyford
This was one of the stations designed by Brunel in 1846/7.

King's Sutton
Auto train leaving for Kingham. Known as the 'Chippy car' by local railwaymen, this service started from the 'up' bay platform at Banbury. The locomotive is one of the 517 Class and the autocar is No. 11 of the B type, a 70 ft vehicle of 1905. Up to 76 passengers could be seated, although it is doubtful if the train ever got that full, except on Banbury market day.

Banbury
The old station with the overall roof. Under the station roof beyond the platform, left, was the bay where the 'Chippy Flyer' auto train departed for Chipping Norton.

Banbury
Ye Olde Reine Deer was typical of the ancient inns that once abounded in the town. Fortunately, the building, including the strange inn sign, survives much as seen here in this mid-1930s picture.

Banbury
Away from the busy station, Banbury town changed very little over the years before the Second World War. This is Parsons Street with the distinctive sign of the Reine Deer Hotel. Hook Norton Ales were (and still are) famous for their quality.

Banbury
An important market town and trading centre between the industrial Midlands and the Oxfordshire Cotswolds. For centuries the town had a wide variety of shops to serve not only its own inhabitants but the rural population in the region unofficially known as 'Banburyshire'. The Elizabethan and Jacobean buildings gave Banbury a distinct flavour in the days when this picture was taken in 1878. The shop on the left is Betts, a popular baker and one of two firms specialising in Banbury Cakes. Obviously shoplifting was no problem for the ironmongers Neale and Fellows – just look at their wares displayed at the edge of the pavement!

Oxford to Worcester

Viewing the North Oxfordshire countryside from the vantage point of our imaginary balloon, we see another railway running north from Oxford, but diverging a couple of miles beyond the city edge to go north-westwards through the delightful countryside of the Cherwell valley. This was the Oxford, Worcester & Wolverhampton Railway – now the main line to Evesham, Worcester and Hereford. It was a line born in the early days of railway expansion through the Cotswolds. The planning, proposals and legal battles (particularly over whether the railway should be built to broad, standard or mixed gauge), lasted over a long period of years in the 1840s and 50s. The main theme of the legal battle was that the Great Western did not want the London & North Western Railway or any company associated with it, coming down to Oxford and thus threatening its Broad Gauge territory.

The Oxford, Worcester & Wolverhampton Railway obtained its Act to build a line from Oxford in 1845. The line was constructed for Broad Gauge trains and all went well until the summer of 1846, when the contractors building the tunnel near Chipping Campden (William Ackroyd and Price) got into financial difficulties and a new contractor had to be found. The new firm, Marchant, progressed work to a fairly advanced state on the tunnel and its approaches before work stopped again because the OW&WR owed £4,300. Again there was another delay in June 1851 over finance, so that the OW&WR decided that they had had enough of Marchant, and handed over the works to the famous firm of Peto and Betts. But Marchant's men stood guard on the works and Brunel (the OW&WR's engineer) arrived on 20 July 1851 with three hundred hefty navvies. Prompt action by the police and a double reading of the Riot Act stopped any violence. A few days later Marchant's men went to Campden tunnel, but fortunately decided that, as they were outnumbered (100 men against Peto and Betts' 2,000), they would withdraw. Peace at length reigned and the tunnel was finally completed in 1852.

The GWR was very annoyed in 1851, when the OW&WR began talks with the LNWR about the possibility of the line becoming a standard gauge one, so that LNWR and even Midland Railway trains could reach Oxford. It should be mentioned that the LNWR already had a Bletchley-Bicester-Oxford line which had opened in 1854. Eventually the OW&WR was laid out as a single track mixed gauge railway, although its own trains were standard gauge and it is said that the Broad Gauge was only used for the Board of Trade Inspection train.

Now came years of financial difficulties and a deterioration in services (hence the 'Old Worse and Worse' tag). Locomotives and the rolling stock declined in efficiency and it was fairly common for trains to be hours late.

On 1 July 1860, the railway, with the Newport, Abergavenny & Hereford Railway formed themselves into the West Midland Railway, which was in turn absorbed by the Great Western on 1 August 1863.

At the height of steam days, there were stations between Oxford and Honeybourne: Yarnton; Handborough, Charlbury; Ascott-under-Wychwood; Shipton; Kingham, originally called Chipping Norton Junction; Adlestrop; Moreton-in-Marsh; Blockley; Campden and Honeybourne, later the junction for the Stratford to Cheltenham via Broadway line. The railway then crossing over the Vale of Evesham to Worcester. The effect brought about by the line (despite its early record of unreliability) was increased prosperity for the small towns through which it passed.

At Moreton-in-Marsh, for example, the local newspaper *The Moreton Free Press* (founded 1850) was soon being read in the neighbouring towns of Chipping Campden, Shipton and Blockley the same day, the copies being sent by train. It was towns like Moreton, which had been described earlier in the decade as, 'a curious half forsaken old town', which began to liven up, and their cattle and sheep markets prospered now that stock could be moved quickly by train.

The new railway also brought industry. At Blockley, the local economy was improved by the principal local landowner, Sir James Rushout of Northwick Park, when he introduced the silk process known as 'throwsting'. The silk was sent to Blockley by train from Coventry and the villagers twisted the silk into threads before it was then returned to the silk mills of the Midlands. At one stage some 3,000 local people were employed in the work. But eventually the industry failed when cheap silk imports from Japan flooded the markets.

One of the more remote stations along the line was Chipping Norton Junction, later Kingham. It was from this place, midway between the villages of Kingham and Bledington, that a branch line was built to Chipping Norton. But before we descend in our imaginary balloon and take a look at that line, here is a description by Edward Madgewick of a journey made as a small boy from London to Moreton-in-Marsh on the OW&WR. It took place in the 1920s when the 1.45pm from Paddington was known as the 'Tea-Time' train and the 4.45pm 'The Slip'. It was to the later train that Edward Madgewick and his parents made their way:

As we were travelling to Moreton, the ticket collector would take special care to indicate the position of the slip coach. This was at the front of the last four or five coaches, which would later be detached at Oxford, where they would form the 6.10pm slow to Worcester.

The train moved off and

. . . now we could recognize landmarks even in the dark. Past Wolvercote Junction and onto our own Worcester line. We seemed to be going faster now. Handborough flashed past, Charlbury, Ascot, Shipton, Bruern Crossing (always recognisable) and the rush through Kingham, Adlestrop hard to notice, but we always knew when we were in the final straight as we approached the Moreton 'distant' and then, just before the Croft, a sense of brakes going on, a noticeable jerk and we were slipped.

A gathering up of belongings, under the London Road bridge past the black shape of the old goods shed, and then we were there, actually at Moreton, and enjoying a warm welcome that always awaited us . . .

Enstone *(top right)*
One of the City of Oxford Motor services solid-tyred Daimlers in the village centre. The children have turned out to see the smart new bus. The Oxford Company absorbed many of the smaller firms in the 1920s, including those of William Payne and Son, (founded 1852) who operated from Oxford to Banbury, Eynsham, Woodstock and Chipping Norton from 1913.

Charlbury *(bottom right)*
Travel on the roads was dangerous even in the days when there was less motor traffic. This bus has come to grief near Charlbury, partly demolishing a Cotswold stone wall. The accident is recorded as having taken place on 14 September 1929.

The Old Worse And Worse
Very early photograph with train approaching Oxford soon after the track was converted from Broad Gauge to standard gauge.

ENSTONE. 21

Charlbury
This delightful study was titled 'The Bus Terminus'. It dates from the early 1920s and shows one of the City of Oxford Motor Services' Daimlers outside the post office. Luggage and goods from the market could be stowed for passengers on the roof of the vehicle.

Enstone
Oxford bus waiting for passengers in the village about 1951.

Charlbury
A Worcester bound express in about 1910. Note the small gas works on the right. To the left there is the usual busy goods yard serving a wide area of this part of Oxfordshire.

Ascot Under Wychwood
This view shows the station as it was in the Edwardian high noon of railways, with a GWR local goods train waiting for the signal.

Kingham
The station was a busy place in the 1900s. Here passengers are changing from the Banbury via Chipping Norton train, right, to the Oxford and Paddington train.

Local trains came off the main Banbury to Cheltenham line to call at Kingham (then named Chipping Norton Junction) before resuming their journeys.

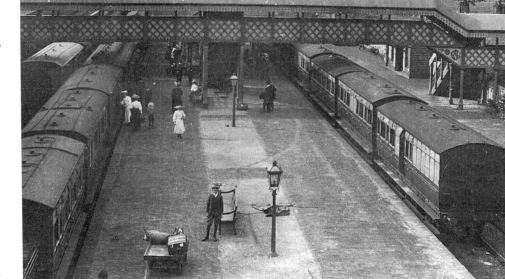

Kingham
The original name of this Cotswold Junction was Chipping Norton Junction. The building on the left-hand side was the Langston Arms Hotel which at one time was connected by an extension of the station footbridge. Next to the hotel was a small cattle market. Amazingly, both enterprises lasted until recent years.

Kingham
The Paddington-Worcester express about to depart in the late 1950s. The rather ugly station buildings here were eventually demolished.

Adlestrop
The Worcester express speeds through whilst the station staff pose for the photographer. This was the station that not long before this picture was taken had been immortalised by Edward Thomas in his poem *I Remember Adlestrop*.

Moreton-in-Marsh
AEC type rail car (known as a 'Flying Banana') arriving on the 'down' platform in the 1950s. The railcars were popular for intermediate services on the OW&WR.

Moreton-in-Marsh
Looking northwards Worcester and Evesham, with AEC rail car. Over to the left beyond the station buildings were the stables for the horses used on the Moreton-Stratford Railway of 1829. Horse power was used because it was felt that it was more reliable than the steam locomotives then available.

Chipping Campden tunnel
The tunnel is actually situated near Mickleton and was the scene of violence between rival contractor's gangs in the 1890s. In this view repair work is in progress. The strange looking pieces of wood are probably used for checking the curvature of the tunnel lining.

Chipping Campden
This was one of the few stations on the line with a level crossing. The small station had sidings for the handling of local 'exports', which included gloves and tweed cloth in the early years of this century.

Chipping Campden High Street
When the railway first opened Chipping Campden was in decline. It was T. Ashbee and his band of craftsmen who settled in the town and restored the buildings, so that G. M. Trevelyn described the town as 'The most beautiful village street now left in the island'. In the railway rationalisation of the 1960s, Chipping Campden lost its railway station and trains now speed past the overgrown site.

Honeybourne
Here is locomotive No. 4999 *Gospel Hall* waiting with a freight train for Oxford on 5 June 1962, ready for the assistance of a banking engine to take the train up the gradients to Chipping Campden. The station closed on 5 May 1969, when services finally ceased on the Stratford section for passenger trains. But there was a welcome revival on the Worcester line thanks to the efforts of the Cotswold Line Promotion Group and large crowds turned up for the official re-opening ceremony on 22 May 1981.

Chipping Campden
Steam rail motor about 1908. This vehicle was rebuilt in 1933 as a 77 seat B type trailer and was renumbered 201.

Chipping Campden
The 2 pm Worcester to Paddington express climbing the bank to Chipping Campden tunnel in the summer of 1949. The locomotive is Castle Class No. 5063 *Earl Baldwin*. When this locomotive was completed at Swindon in June 1937, it was named *Thornbury Castle*, but the next month a decision was made to name it after Stanley Baldwin, the former Prime Minister. The engine was withdrawn from service in February 1965.

Banbury to Cheltenham

We have mentioned that Kingham was the junction for a branch line to Chipping Norton in the early days of the OW&WR line. It was this branch that was eventually to form part of the long cross-country railway from a junction with the Oxford-Banbury and Bicester line at King's Sutton, to Cheltenham in the west: a railway that crossed some of the finest Cotswold scenery on its way.

Back in 1821, the Bliss family had come down from the north to settle in the then remote town of Chipping Norton, where they set up a cloth mill so that they were near the sheep that supplied the raw material. Water power was used at first, but technology in the cloth industry was advancing and steam power was becoming the order of the time. It was William Bliss (1810–83) who was to convert his Chipping Norton mill to steam power, but he found that the cost of transporting the coal from the Oxford Canal was expensive. His mill was already gaining a reputation for fine cloth and so he devised a number of schemes with local farmers and businessmen, for a railway to link the town with the OW&WR or to the LNWR at Banbury via the Stour valley.

Bliss approached the LNWR to see if they were interested in a line. Naturally the GWR and the OW&WR were worried and eventually made an offer of help for a line westward to Kingham, as they were not happy about a possible LNWR attempt to enter the Cotswolds. The Chipping Norton Railway Company received its Act in September 1854 and the famous contractor, Sir Morton Peto (1809–89) was engaged to survey and build the line, assisted by John (later Sir John) Fowler. The line was opened on 10 August 1855, after less than a year's work. The day was a public holiday in Chipping Norton and a 'considerable number of respectable inhabitants of the locality were congregated at the railway station, which was decorated with evergreens and banners besides other indications of pleasures appropriate to the occasion'. Apparently the banners bore the somewhat curious message: 'Unrestricted Commerce', whilst others had the wording 'The People's Friend' or 'Extension of Education'. One wonders if they had been left over from an election campaign!

The official opening train was hauled by the locomotive *Eugene* named after the then very popular Empress of France. William Bliss had won a prize of £500 at the Great Exhibition of 1851, the award being given by the French Emperor to the British company which had done the most for its workers' welfare.

The special train reached Chipping Norton at 1pm to the cheers of a large assembly of people. A great celebration lunch was held at the Town Hall, the catering being in the hands of The White Hart Hotel. 'The dinner was of a sumptuous character and the wine (port, sherry and champagne) exceptional,' according to a local newspaper. Personalities present included William Bliss, the Mayor, and Sir Morton and Lady Peto. There were four courses, each offering a wide choice of dishes ranging from roast beef and lamb, curried rabbit, goose and duck, to cabinet pudding, plum pudding, gooseberries, plums, raisins and cherries.

Coal could now be carried cheaply to Bliss Mills and the enterprise prospered. By 1864 there were plans to extend the line east to Banbury by way of Hook Norton and King's Sutton and the existing Oxford-Banbury main line. Hook Norton and the area nearby were then becoming important for the mining of ironstone and the new railway would prosper with the carrying of the materials to the industry of the Midlands. But although the Act for the line was passed in 1875, it was not until 1887 that the trains began to run from Chipping Norton to Banbury.

There were several major engineering works on the line, including the 750 yard tunnel just outside the re-sited Chipping Norton station (the old one then became the goods station), and the Hook Norton viaducts. Hook Norton, although a small place, was noted for its flourishing brewery. It was founded by a local farmer John Harris who had begun brewing at his farm in 1849. The Hook Norton brewery soon became famous for the quality of its beer. Harris later built a brewery building in what is described as 'Chinese style' and his 'Hookey Ale' soon became famous in North Oxfordshire – a delight that can still be had today. When the railway came, the ales were then sent over great distances. But beer and farming were not the only industries of the Hook Norton area. Ironstone quarries grew in importance towards the end of the Victorian era. Hook Norton, Adderbury and Bloxham were all places where the material was obtained, and the railway gained much valuable traffic. Ironstone quarrying tended to be more spasmodic after the First World War, the summit of activity being 1918-1942 and 1947-1954. The Brymbo Ironworks was established in 1896, and the Oxfordshire Ironstone Company operated until 1967. The railway was doubled between King's Sutton junction and Hook Norton in 1906 to cater for the extra mineral traffic.

With the opening of the railway from Chipping Norton to Banbury came increases in passenger traffic, and visitors began to discover the delights of the Oxfordshire Cotswolds. At Chipping Norton, the station forecourt would be crowded with horse cabs and small boys, who offered to carry baggage up to the town. Hotels such as The White Hart had their own 'conveyances'. Apparently, it was the custom of the small boys to hang on the back of the loaded carriages and carts as they trundled up the hill to the town. People walking along

would then cry out to the drivers, 'Whip behind; whip behind,' so that the lads would receive a nasty swish of the horse whip, making them let go! Parcels sent by rail would at one time have been collected by Frederick Heath, who had a donkey cart. The GWR also operated a parcels delivery service, first by horse drawn cart, then supplemented by a smart motor lorry in the 1930s.

The westward extension of the railway from Kingham took place in 1862, first to Bourton-on-the-Water, and then to Andoversford where it was later joined by the Midland & South Western Junction Railway. Trains eventually could run right through from Banbury to Cheltenham by means of an avoiding line at Kingham, but local trains called at Kingham, reversing again to rejoin the main line via loop connections.

The opening of this through route enabled trains from far afield to use the line. The Great Central Railway, in conjunction with the GWR began the *Port to Port Express*. It ran from Newcastle to Cardiff via the GCR at Banbury. A further avoiding line near Cheltenham enabled the express to run straight down to Gloucester. The operating practice was to run the train with GWR carriages one day and GCR the

next. It appears that travellers preferred the GCR train, where even the Third class was superior to the First on the GWR stock.

At one time the Banbury to Cheltenham line was called the 'longest branch line in England' by railway journalists. Certainly, (despite the main line expresses) it still retained the leisurely aspect of the rural railway, partly because it ran through no major towns.

After the First World War there were already distant signs that the line was beginning to feel competition from more speedy routes – and by road transport. In 1932 the local train service had been reduced to two trains a day each way from Kingham to Cheltenham, with four trains a day to Banbury. But in 1947, the service was slightly improved when the trains were worked by a GWR 'Flying Banana' diesel railcar. The line closed to passenger trains between Banbury and Chipping Norton on 1 December 1962, goods traffic from 1 December 1965. The Kingham to Cheltenham section closed in 1962.

Kings Sutton
Auto train at King's Sutton with two freight vans at the rear. The auto train service ran as far as Kingham. There was another local service from Kingham to Cheltenham. The carriage here is No. 35 of 1906, with a 517 Class locomotive.

Adderbury
The platforms have already begun to
succumb to nature in this 1967 picture. The
stationmaster's house is seen on the right,
with the view looking towards King's
Sutton.

Bloxham
View in the 1930s. The milk churns on the
platform trolley were once a familiar sight
at rural stations before the days of milk
tanker wagons.

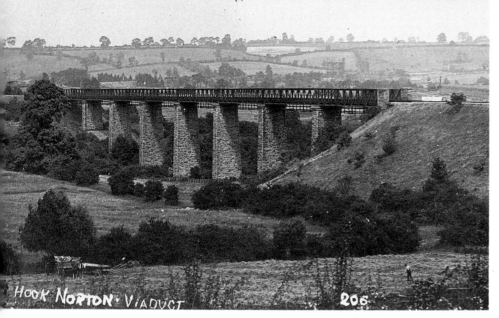

Hook Norton

This was one of the two viaducts between Hook Norton and Great Rollright. The spans were 90 ft high in places and the structure took four years to build, the contractors employing 400 men on the task. Now their work has been destroyed and only parts of the once proud arches remain.

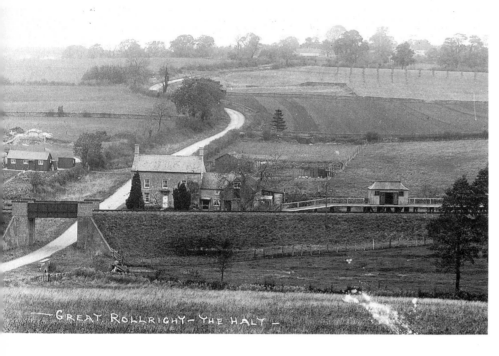

Great Rollright

A typical GWR halt, complete with its iron 'pagoda' shelter. In the 1900s there was a great awakening to the beauties and antiquities of the Cotswolds and the GWR advertised this halt for the nearby ancient stone circle known as the Rollright Stones. At Chipping Norton or Hook Norton nearby, one could buy 'Six real Photos in a packet of sketches of the Rollright Stones with legends'. They were published by the local photographer Percy Simms & Son for two shillings (10p).

Great Rollright

This picture was reproduced from an old postcard from Hook Norton in 1906. The message on the back says that the house by the road in the centre of the picture was occupied at that time by a Mr and Mrs Hicks, who were moving to Birmingham. Perhaps the remoteness of the spot, despite the local trains, was too much and Mrs Hicks yearned for the trappings of Edwardian town life – gas lighting, piped water, a choice of shops, and frequent electric trams to take them to the Birmingham music hall on a Saturday evening.

Hook Norton

The Brymbo ironstone plant, showing the gas-fired kilns for calcining the ironstone. They were fed by a network of 2 ft gauge lines from the nearby quarries. The lines were worked by Hudswell Clarke saddle tank locomotives *Gwen* and *Jean*. The plant was in operation from 1896-1926, but there were some local ironstone workings until the early 1970s.

Hook Norton

Though never as important as its neighbour Chipping Norton, Hook Norton was larger than just a village, although not quite a town. In the middle of the nineteenth century, its brewery was started by a local farmer and still flourishes, the well-loved 'Hookey ales' being enjoyed in a wide area of Oxfordshire. This is the brewery, photographed early this century.

HOOK NORTON
THE RAILWAY STATION

Hook Norton

The station staff, proud of their gardens and neat platforms, have turned out to see the photographer. They did not know that later in the century, the line would be closed, the tracks torn up and little would be left of their way of life.

Hook Norton

When Sir Sam Fay became general manager of the Great Central he developed a useful network of cross-country services, encouraging other railways to run their trains along his tracks. This is the Cardiff-Newcastle express passing through the station, with Great Central carriages specially built for this route. They provided a high degree of comfort and it must have been pleasant on some Edwardian spring day to sit back against the plush upholstery and watch the rolling Cotswolds hurry by. The locomotive here is Great Western. Engines were changed at Banbury, the train continuing over the GCR's line. On alternate days the train would be composed of GWR stock.

CARDIFF TO NEWCASTLE EXPRESS PASSING HOOK NORTON STATION.

Hook Norton
The goods shed beyond and the Railway Inn behind was the first of the two spectacular viaducts – constructed of steel girders resting on 90 feet high stone piers. Although the railway has gone, these massive stone columns still survive.

Chipping Norton
Edwardian elegance as well-dressed passengers wait for the Kingham and Cheltenham train. This is the new station opened in 1887 when the branch was extended to King's Sutton and the main Banbury line. Behind the station is the goods yard on the site of the original terminus of 1855.

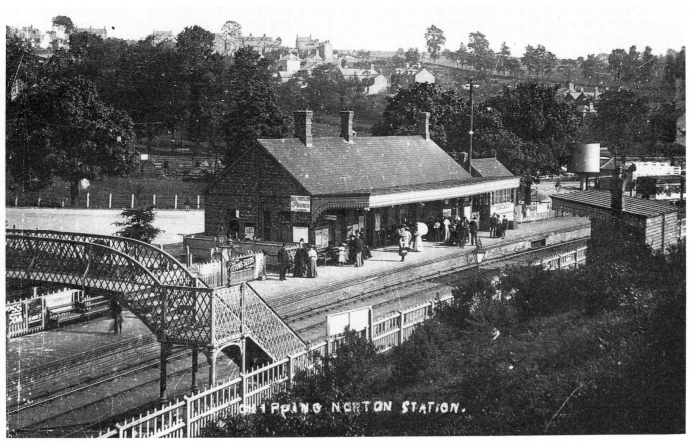

THE ACCIDENT ON THE LINE AT CHIPPING NORTON

Chipping Norton
Mishap in the goods yard by the old West Box, with 500 Class No. 546 in difficulties with a Wolverhampton based brake van.

Chipping Norton
The station in about 1911, looking towards Kingham and the goods yards. This was perhaps the most picturesque station on the line from King's Sutton to Kingham.

CHIPPING NORTON. RAILWAY STATION.

Chipping Norton
Almost every station in the Cotswolds had local firms with their own wagons. This one was built by the Gloucester Carriage & Wagons Co in February 1900, and was painted black.

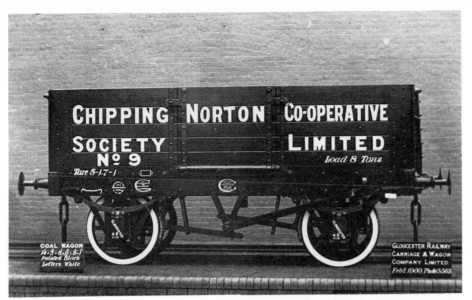

Chipping Norton
A rather fanciful view of William Bliss's Tweed Mills just outside the town when they were rebuilt in the classical North of England style in 1851.

Chipping Norton
This picture was taken sometime before the First World War. The road is The Leys and many of the houses were built by the GWR for local railway staff. The two wagons on the right belong to Bliss Tweed Mill and were used for conveying coal to the mill buildings, a half mile or so further up the line.

Chipping Norton
Looking along Middle Row to the Market
Place, with the eighteenth century town
hall in the distance. The centre building in
the terrace over to the left by the tree, is
the White Hart Hotel which was a centre
of social life. This picture was reproduced
from a postcard mailed in February 1912,
but the photograph was probably older
than this.

The evacuees
A very long train arriving at Chipping
Norton. It is filled with children evacuated
with great speed from London during the
last days before the outbreak of war in
September 1939. For most children, their
first glimpse of the Cotswolds and of the
countryside was from the train as it
steamed up the line from Banbury.
Billeting, which had been done with haste,
still left most children feeling hopelessly
lost at first, although attempts were made
to keep children of one family unit
together. It was a hit-or-miss affair, but in
general, the kind country people coped
well, although they found it difficlt to deal
with town children, who were used to
spending their spare days in the streets.

Getting the mail through
The heavy fall of snow has not prevented anyone from enjoying this work – perhaps because many hands make light work. A scene from Edwardian days.

Deep midwinter
Near Chipping Norton with a City of Oxford bus in the bitter weather of 1947. Often it was the railways which provided the only link with the outside world.

Flying High
An aircraft flies upside down over the waiting two-engined biplane *Queen Hunter*. Cobham used this and his airliner *Youth of Britain* to give flights to civic dignitaries and members of the public, as well as giving local lectures on flying. Mr Cannon, a local man told us:

> The flight took off from a local farm on the Banbury Road, with Sir Alan piloting the plane from an open cockpit set just behind the passenger cabin and on a higher level so that he could see over the wings and engines. None of us had flown, apart from 3 minute flips in the smaller 'circus' Avros. The stunts were the talk of the town, and on Whit Monday there was 'wing walking'; they also 'bombed' the town with bags containing confetti.

Volunteers
King George VI inspects local forces, including the Home Guard, on a cold day early in the Second World War at Chipping Norton. The Home Guard could always be relied on to find enemy airmen who had escaped by landing safely by parachute. On one occasion a German aircraft member escaped thus and walked along a lane and stopped a bus, calmly got aboard, and gave himself up to two rather flabbergasted guardians of the Empire who thought themselves off duty at the time!

Stow

The market town stands on its hill, a good steep mile from the station which must have been taxing for older people especially in winter. The station building was rebuilt in the 1930s in the Cotswold style. Today, following closure, it is a private house. Even the row of fir trees has survived.

Stow

At 475 ft above sea level, Stow-on-the-Wold station was almost as windy a place as the town.

Stow

The horse fair in 1905 with lines of animals at the side of the Foss Way. There is an interesting assortment of agricultural equipment in the foreground. Horses gradually succeeded sheep in importance at Stow. Today, there are two annual horse fairs, now held in nearby fields.

Bourton

These are the original buildings of 1899 that were replaced by a Cotswold style building in the 1920s. There is a lot of activity in this picture, a train for Cheltenham is at the 'down' platform, whilst goods train shunting is taking place on the 'up' line. There were goods sidings here, and coal merchants included C. Collett & Sons and George Clifford, both having their own wagons.

Andoversford

This was a place that became important for trade after the Cheltenham-Banbury and M&SWJ lines arrived. A weekly market was set up in the last nineteenth century. The building here is the Andoversford Hotel. The signboard in the Centre of the picture is for the famous Dursley firm of R. A. Lister, and they are no doubt selling their gas-oil engines to the more enlightened local farmers. Shown here is a good cross section of Cotswold rural folk in pre-1914 days.

Dowdeswell Viaduct
After leaving the Sandywell Park Tunnel, the line emerged from a wooded cutting onto the viaduct. Widened to take the trains of the Midland & South Western Junction Railway, it crossed the river Chelt. The quiet highway in the foreground is now the A40 trunk road from London to Cheltenham.

Cheltenham Spa, St James Station
The old GWR and M&SWJR joint terminus in St James Square. It was the most conveniently sited of the Cheltenham stations. Tennyson used to live nearby and would sometimes stroll over and talk to a pet parrot by the station offices. Apparently the bird could recite the destinations of the trains more distinctly than the station staff.

Cheltenham

Opening day of the GWR bus service from St James Station to Oxford on 29 October 1928. The contemporary advertisements announced 'New Road Conveyance' in conjunction with the Paddington to Oxford rail services. The average journey time was 3 to 4 hours. The vehicle seen here is one of the Thorneycroft coaches.

Cheltenham coach station

When this picture was taken in 1937, Black & White Motorways were operating a network of services from Cheltenham to all parts of the country. The company started in 1926, with a daily service along the A40 to London, leaving Cheltenham at 8.45 am and reaching London at 2 pm. There was an early return journey at 2 pm, because in winter it was felt that many passengers would not want to travel along the dark and dangerous roads. The vehicles used at this time were 8-cylinder Pullman Record coaches, seating 21 people. The London terminus was at West Kensington station.

In 1928, the London terminus was moved to Hammersmith Broadway, where the Black & White Co opened offices. It was H. R. Lapper, the new general manager appointed in 1928, who expanded the company. The old Regency house in this picture was soon surrounded by a spacious coach station, with café and all facilities. The old house was destroyed in the war, but the coach station continues to flourish.

Braving the floods
All was not always plain sailing on the old A40. A Black & White coach makes a dash through the water near Cheltenham. The luggage is safe and dry under the canvas covering up on the roof.

Cheltenham
The Promenade, the centre of the town's fashionable shops. Even in 1938 there seems little danger of traffic jams. The Cadena Cafe on the left, just to the rear of the car, was a popular rendezvous for morning coffee or afternoon tea. On the extreme left are the showrooms of Dale Forty & Co, where you could buy a piano to grace the drawing room of your Regency house at Pitteville or Lansdown. The Black & White Coach Co had a travel office to the right of the cafe until recent times.

THE PROMENADE, CHELTENHAM.   K.1723

The Midland & South Western Junction

Let us now imagine that our balloon journey has brought us to Cirencester, the ancient capital of the Cotswolds. We have already seen how the town was linked by the GWR branch from Kemble in 1841. But later in the century, it became an important place on a line from Swindon Town to Cheltenham across the loneliest part of the Cotswolds. The story of Victorian railway enterprise is full of struggles by small companies with grand visions of expansion, but under capitalised and short of traffic. Many of these companies were usually quickly absorbed by the larger ones – particularly in the country served by the mighty Great Western. The fact that the tiny M&SWJ survived until the grouping of 1922, right in the middle of GWR territory, is a remarkable story.

The M&SWJ's origins lay in proposals for a Manchester to Southampton railway in 1845 – a scheme that met with considerable opposition. Eventually, the promoters obtained an Act for a railway from Andover (and the London & South Western Railway) to Swindon Town in 1881. There was much opposition from the Great Western, because it considered the line was an invasion of its own country. The Swindon, Marlborough & Andover Railway had its headquarters at Swindon Town, the station being built in Devizes Road, well south of the New Town and the GWR. In the same year, the Swindon & Cheltenham Extension Railway Act was passed and the church bells were rung in Cricklade and Cirencester churches to celebrate

the event. The line was completed between Swindon Town and Cirencester in 1883, and in the same year the two companies were amalgamated to form the Midland & South Western Junction Railway. But the new company, having already been formed from two under-financed concerns, soon got into financial difficulties and there was trouble in raising the capital for the extension from Cirencester to Cheltenham to form the Midland Railway. Work on the line north of Cirencester encountered some difficult country, particularly the boring of the Chedworth Tunnel and the M&SWJR was unable to pay the contractors at one stage. The Metropolitan Carriage & Wagon Company, who had supplied the rolling stock, threatened to take possession of the carriages unless immediate payment was made. It is said that a watchman was employed at Swindon Town to prevent the carriages being spirited away in the night.

However, eventually the money was raised to pay off debts, and to pay for the extension to Cheltenham; the contractors planned to have the line completed by 24 May 1890. Then disaster struck at Chedworth, when part of the tunnel brickwork collapsed followed by an earth fall, so that a hole appeared in the fields above. The Railway was forced to take legal action before the contactor would repair the damage. It was early in 1891 before the first trains ran through to Cheltenham, after delays due to severe winter weather, and

July before passenger services commenced.

The M&SWJR seemed doomed to financial collapse, but was saved by the appointment of Sam Fay, later to gain fame as the Chairman of the Great Central Railway. Fay arrived at the Swindon Town offices on 16 March 1891 to be told that there was no money to pay the wages for that week. But Fay was undeterred: 'Don't say that,' he told the Company Secretary, 'I see great possibilities for this line'.

In the next few years Fay transformed the M&SWJR from an ailing concern into a flourishing cross-country railway. Goods traffic was increased by 73%, James Tyrell was appointed locomotive superintendent in 1903, and it was his smart express locomotives, running with refurbished ex-Midland Railway carriages, that provided a popular service from Southampton to Cheltenham. At the same time, Tyrell established his locomotive and carriage and wagon works at Cirencester.

Great attention was now paid to freight traffic and almost every station was provided with a siding to serve the local farming communities. Typical was the remote station at Foss Cross, north of Cirencester. Arthur Gibbs in his book *A Cotswold Village* (1898) said of this part of the Cotswolds:

> A country which is never explored by the artist, far from the railways and the busy haunts of men, not even mentioned in the guide books.'

The coming of the M&SWJR

changed all that.

Four years ago, with a small station at Foss Cross, there were many inhabitants of these old world villages who had never seen a train or railway.

Now these people could have a day out savouring the sophistication of Cheltenham or the market at Cirencester.

During the two world wars, the M&SWJR carried very heavy freight traffic and innumerable military trains. There was a steady stream of troop trains heading south and a sad number of ambulance specials steaming north. These were the days when the line saw a very wide variety of rolling stock. The carriages of the Scottish railways (such as the Caledonian, North British and Highland) mingled with the less rare North Eastern, LNWR and Midland. Locomotives were drafted in from other railways to cope with the traffic and there were extra sidings laid out at various places on the route.

In peace time, local passenger traffic was to become increasingly scarce as the motor bus gained ground. But products such as milk were still important. At Cricklade it is recorded that 12,000 gallons were dispatched daily. There was a special M&SWJR milk train that began its long run south from here, the 2¼cwt churns being handled at each station down to Marlborough and Andover by the station staff. The train eventually reached London at Clapham Junction or Waterloo, in the early hours of the morning; a far cry from the Cotswolds and the Wiltshire Downs. It was said that in the 1920s the slowest train in Britain was the 5pm milk train from Cricklade to Andover on Sundays. It took nearly three hours to run the 31 miles.

With the grouping of the railways in 1923, the Great Western took over and began changes almost at once. The works at Cirencester were closed and gradually the company's engines and carriages were replaced by GWR rolling stock. In 1936 one of the first GWR diesel rail car services was introduced between Cheltenham and Swindon Town and speeds of 60mph were recorded. But there was little support from the public and later the familiar tank engines and B set carriages were used. The main line through services were reasonably patronised, whilst suburban service was inaugurated between the old M&SWJR station at Swindon Town and the GWR at Swindon Junction via the connecting curve at Rushey Platt. One of the authors can vividly remember taking a lunch time trip on this service during the war years, using sparse pocket money!

Memories, too, of war-time troop trains, especially those loaded with GI's, who would sometimes throw out packets of Camel cigarettes and even the odd can of tinned fruit to the trainspotters at Hay Lane bridge, Swindon.

The end of the line was in sight when the trains were diverted from Cheltenham Lansdown Station to St. James in 1958, so that through main line trains could no longer be handled. The local service was uneconomic and the railway began to die. Express goods trains ceased, leaving only local 'pickups' which were always threatened by road delivery services. Passenger trains ceased in 1961, the line being completely closed north of Cirencester (Watermoor). Freight traffic survived between Swindon Town and Cirencester for another year.

The ghost of the M&SWJR took a long time finally to go. In the early 1970s trains carrying stone and materials for the building of the M4 motorway south of Swindon were worked round through Swindon Town. All has not finally gone. The Swindon & Cricklade Railway Society are rebuilding a section of the old line near Blunsdon and it is possible to see a steam train again running on a short section of the old line.

Swindon Town
The station was the headquarters of the original section of the line – the Swindon, Marlborough & Andover Railway, which subsequently formed the Midland & South Western Junction Railway. The buildings to the right in the background were the company offices. In its early days, the M&SWJR also had its locomotive and carriage works here, but due to a very cramped site, they were eventually moved north to Cirencester. Swindon Town station, which was situated on the south side of Old Swindon Hill, opened on 27 July 1881 and possibly this photograph was taken either that day or soon afterwards.

Swindon Town
A busy scene in the late 1900s as the *Cheltenham* or *North Express* from Southampton is about to leave. The original station of 1881 was enlarged and the Cheltenham platform made into an island in 1907. This picture is taken from Croft Road bridge.

Swindon Town
The *Cheltenham-Southampton Express* in British Railways days. The train services on the railway had already begun their slow but sure decline to final closure ten years later. But despite the busy station at Swindon Town, which at one time even boasted refreshment rooms, the general atmosphere on the M&SWJR was one of rural slumber. In his book *The Thames*

Fred S. Thacker wrote:
That curious, patient line, the Midland & South Western Junction . . . remote, unfriended, melancholy, slow, which by gentle processes connects Birmingham with Southampton . . . I have used it several times, invariably at the expense of much waiting. Indeed, I got into talk once with a man going south, who being nearly two hours late, congratulated me, going north, upon my delay of less than an hour.

Cricklade

Goods train entering the station about 1910. There was a great deal of activity at Cricklade before 1939 and the amazing total of 12,000 gallons of milk daily came from the surrounding farms. It was usually conveyed in 2¼ cwt churns. They were man-handled onto the trains by the staff, who had to have a strong physique to move each churn with its 71 gallons of Wiltshire milk. The trains went all the way to Andover and then up the L&SWR (London and South Western Railway) to Clapham or Waterloo. On Sundays, at one time, the mixed train took three hours for the 41 mile journey down to Andover from Cricklade!

South Cerney

The station was originally called Cerney & Ashton Keynes. The train is hauled by a 2-6-0 Beyer Peacock locomotive of 1897, No. 16. In 1925 she was transferred by the GWR to the Bristol region and scrapped in 1930. The approaching passenger train is hauled by one of the 2-4-0 locomotives supplied to the railway by Dubs in 1894.

South Cerney
Sad day at Cerney in 1962: the last passenger trains have gone and the rusty track sees only the occasional goods train.

Cirencester
When Sir Sam Fay took over the running of the M&SWJR in 1895, he moved the offices of the company to Cirencester, where the works were established. This picture was taken in 1906, possibly to record a visit by the Directors. The locomotive, probably No. 5, is one of the 2-4-0s built in 1881.

Cirencester
An Edwardian summer afternoon and a horse drawn vehicle rattles gently towards the M&SWJR station at Watermoor.

Listen to the Band!
History has recorded how well the M&SWJR's staff band performed. However, we can be sure that they were enthusiastic, especially when their chairman and patron, Sam Fay was present. The staff band, as part of the Cirencester Works Sports & Social Club, existed until the First World War.

Cirencester
One of the M&SWJR's 4-4-0 locomotives built by the North British Loco Co in 1909, standing with a cattle wagon in the yard at Cirencester before the First World War. This engine, No. 42 was withdrawn by the GWR in 1931. The last of the class survived until December 1938.

Cirencester
Looking north towards Andoversford. The last passenger trains have gone and the advertisements have been removed. Only the single goods track remains, the shadow of Dr Beeching growing ever more darkly over the site.

Cirencester
Looking towards the former railway works about 1961. The M&SWJR moved its locomotive, carriage and wagon works from Swindon, where there was insufficient land available, to Cirencester in the autumn of 1895. The locomotive superintendent, James Tyrell, and the company's general manager, Sir Sam Fay had their offices here. Extensions were made to the works in 1903 and 1915. Closed by the GWR in 1925, the staff were transported every day to Swindon Junction by a special train which left Cirencester at 6.47 am.

Cirencester
The view south after withdrawal of passenger services. Extensive sidings once served the gas works. The building nearest the camera was the Permanent Way Inspector's office. Originally this corrugated iron building had been the stationmaster's home, then Tyrell's office. Connal, at one time the company civil engineer, had a drawing office in the building.

Foss Cross station
A place of importance on the line, even though it was miles from anywhere. There were sidings for handling farm produce and for bringing in supplies and it was, therefore, a convenient stop for farmers. There were no fewer than three coal merchants. The line was doubled from 12 July 1901, the finance being partly supplied by the Midland Railway. During the Second World War there was a story that a signal man kept rabbits beneath the signal box floor to supplement his income.

Foss Bridge
Surely this picture is the very essence of those classic days of thirties motoring. Then Shell Mex was 1/3d (approx 7p) a gallon, and inns, like the one seen here had begun to cater for motorists, with comfortable dining rooms and bedrooms with central heating.

Chedworth

Everyone has heard of the famous Roman villa, which actually lies north to the village at Yanworth. The M&SWJR was built very close to the villa and Lord Stowell, the land owner, stipulated that construction of the line was not to disturb the remains. The station seen here was the highest on the line (at 637 ft). In the First World War sidings were laid out by the Timber Control Department of the government, using Portuguese labour. Some 1,000 tons of timber were removed from the magnificent Chedworth woods before the venture closed on 30 June 1923.

The building on the right was the village school house. The station was reduced to an unstaffed halt from February 1954. Now the railway has gone and the woods have closed over the embankments and cuttings.

Chedworth tunnel

The preliminary digging work at Chedworth tunnel in 1883, when 480 men and 630 horses with aid of 5 steam navvies worked away in difficult conditions. They lived in a special camp because the spot was miles from anywhere. The 494 yard tunnel partly collapsed and was the subject of a legal dispute between the M&SWJR and the contractor, Charles Braddock.

Andoversford
Looking east towards the junction of the
Banbury line (left) and the M&SWJR
(right) about 1950. The bridge just visible
at the end of the platforms crossed the A40
road to Oxford. There was originally a
separate M&SWJR station called
Andoversford & Doddeswell, but this was
closed on 1 April 1927.

Cheltenham
The South Express near Charlton King's
on its long cross-country journey by single
track to Southampton. The picture dates
from the early 1930s, and the locomotive is
ex-M&SWJR No. 9 4-4-0 built by the
North British Locomotive Co in 1912. She
was withdrawn from service in 1938, as
GWR No. 1123.

The Last Fling
Honeybourne to Cheltenham

As we glide again over the Cotswolds to the far west, we cross the wooded heights of the Western Edge and look down on the Severn Plain and the orchards of the Vale of Evesham. Just where the line from Oxford to Worcester leaves the hills beyond Chipping Campden is a junction station – Honeybourne. Here another line can be seen running at the foot of the hills south westwards towards Cheltenham. This is the Stratford to Cheltenham line, built from Honeybourne at the beginning of this century.

The original section from Stratford to Honeybourne opened in 1859 as part of the Oxford, Wolverhampton & Worcester Railway (the OW&WR). The Great Western, after acquiring that company, had thought of extending the branch to Evesham but nothing was done until the threat of the Andoversford and Stratford railway project arrived in 1898. This was to be a Midland & South Western Junction line. Fortunately for the GWR, the plan was rejected. The Great Western then proposed a line from Honeybourne to Cheltenham to open up country districts previously many miles from a station. Parliamentary powers were obtained in 1899 and work began in late 1902 with contractors Walter Scott and Middleton in charge.

Goods trains began running to Toddington in August 1904, although passenger trains terminated at Broadway until the end of the year as the station buildings were not ready at Toddington. Winchcombe was

reached in February 1905 and Cheltenham in August 1905. The old line from Stratford to Honeybourne, now forming the northern section of the new line, was double-tracked by the end of 1907, making it accessible to through trains from other parts of the country.

Although the line skirted the Cotswolds Edge there were a number of works, including the making up of approaches to carry the main Evesham road over the line near Honeybourne and a 15 arch viaduct near the picturesque village of Stanway. It was during the building of this viaduct that a serious accident happened. Four of the arches collapsed, killing four men and injuring a number of others, in November 1903. It was said that floods caused the disaster, which was further compounded by the weight of a heavy crane on top of the viaduct causing the first of the arches to collapse. The date was Friday the 13th!

The massive bulk of that outcrop of the Cotswolds, Cleeve Hill, faced the builder with either a lengthy tunnel or a diversion. The latter was chosen and the line made a series of curves. A tunnel was required at Greet, where, because of the treacherous nature of the soil, the walls were 2ft.7½ inches thick. There were also some deep cuttings which caused earth stabilization problems. There was a further tunnel near Cheltenham at a place near the race course at Hunting Butts. It was only 97 yards long, but had deep approach cuttings and the contractors removed something

like 22,000 cubic yards of material. In the suburbs of Cheltenham, houses had to be demolished and retaining walls built to the deep cutting before the line reached Malvern Road station. Eventually the works on the line were landscaped and some pleasing plantings of conifer trees carried out.

The stations on the new lines were, from Honeybourne: Weston-sub-Edge, Willersley, Broadway, Laverton Halt, Toddington, Hailes Abbey Halt, Winchcombe, Gratton Halt, Gothrington, Bishop's Cleeve, Cheltenham Race Course and Cheltenham Malvern Road. Many had goods yards and sheds, with facilities for handling the fruit grown in the Vale of Evesham.

With the improvements from Stratford to Honeybourne through express trains began using the route, including services from Birmingham, via Stratford, to Cheltenham; and from Newcastle to Cardiff. The Birmingham to Bristol service began in July 1908, but could hardly call its progress 'express', as it meandered through the peaceful Cotswold Edge country, taking nearly three hours. Eventually trains were extended south westwards to distant Penzance, and it is said that in the 1930s the carriages carried the longest list of places on their destination boards of any line in Britain: Wolverhampton, Birmingham, Stratford-on-Avon, Bristol, Plymouth and Penzance. These trains by-passed Cheltenham itself by means of a connecting spur to the line between Cheltenham and Gloucester.

In 1936, local services included some operated by the streamlined diesel railcars known affectionately as 'Flying Bananas'. The timetables cautioned passengers that 'there was only one Class – limited accommodation'. During the 1920s there was even a train from Paddington to Worcester with a slip carriage bearing the destination 'Cheltenham via Broadway', the carriage being 'slipped' as the Worcester train sped through Moreton-in-Marsh. There were also further 'Flying Banana' trains from Birmingham and Stratford to Cheltenham and Cardiff.

By 1939 decline had set in, and the only remaining through train was the Wolverhampton to Penzance express. It was restored after the war and in 1952 even received a name: *The Cornishman*. In 1960 the local trains between Honeybourne and Cheltenham were withdrawn, but there was still a passenger service to the racecourse station, with specials coming from many parts of the country. Freight trains continued to use the route. The racecourse station finally closed on 21 March 1968, but the line was retained for emergency use and through freight trains. It was one of these – a train to Severn Tunnel Junction working that came to grief at Winchcombe on 25 August 1975. The derailment badly damaged the track and the death knell of the entire railway was sounded. Despite protests, the line was closed with the exception of the Honeybourne-Long Marston single track line, which was used as a long siding.

Today, the line has come alive again at Toddington, where the Gloucestershire Warwickshire Railway Preservation Society has a steam centre and the line is now re-opened to Winchcombe.

Honeybourne
South Wales to Midlands freight at Honeybourne West Juction 3 July 1962, with a Churchward 2-8-0 locomotive. The ridge of the Cotswolds can be seen in the background.

Toddington
A view from the late 1950s with a goods
train in the distance rattling down the tracks
to Cheltenham. The bulk of the Cotswolds
near Cleeve Hill are in the background.
The line made a series of curves around
the steepest heights, although there was
one tunnel, Toddington opened for
passengers and goods on 1 December 1904
– its yards specially designed to handle
fruit trains. Today the station is being
restored as part of the Gloucestershire
Warwickshire Railway Society
headquarters.

Gotherington
Nature is already taking over the deserted
passenger platform in this early 1960s
picture. This station was one of the few on
the Honeybourne-Cheltenham line that
was built in stone.

Bishop's Cleve
Early view with GWR steam rail motor train. The station opened on 1 June 1906 and was the temporary terminus of the Honeybourne line until the Cheltenham station at Malvern Road was ready later the same year.

Cheltenham Race Course
The long platforms and their special steel barriers were designed to handle the vast crowds of race goers – particularly in Gold Cup week. There were no sidings here for the special trains, which were held down the line in Bishop's Cleve. Special trains continued to use this station until 21 March 1968.

Cheltenham Malvern Road
This station was on the line to Cheltenham
St James terminus and trains from
Honeybourne joined those from the GWR
Gloucester line and those of the M&SWJR
and Banbury line services.

NEW RAILWAY
FROM CHELTENHAM TO OXFORD.

To the Owners and Occupiers of Property along the Line.

BEWARE OF THE GREAT WESTERN!

THEIR AGENTS

ARE NOW ACTIVELY EMPLOYED

In Calling on the Owners and Occupiers to induce them to join the
Great Western

In Opposing the Line to Oxford.

I warn you against their insidious designs.

Give them no Information or Assistance ;

AND

CAREFULLY AVOID SIGNING ANY PAPER

Presented to you under any pretence whatever.

W. H. GWINNETT.

CHELTENHAM, 27th December, 1852.

Early scheme
Poster produced in 1852 warning local
landowners not to sell their land to the
GWR who were planning a rival line to
Cheltenham.

Eynsham
Although Cassington Halt opened on 9 March 1936, Eynsham as the first proper station on the East Gloucestershire line after it left the OW&WR at Yarnton north of Oxford. The platform seen on the left was added in 1944, and during the Second World War, Eynsham was one of the busiest stations on the branch handling 12,000 tons of freight and 14,000 passengers a year.

South Leigh
Despite its small size, this station was used by 6,000 people in 1920-30 period. The sheds in the distance were used as emergency food stores during the war.

The Witney and East Gloucestershire Railway

As we float eastwards again, one last railway remains for us to look at – the branch from Oxford, which left the Worcester main line at Yarnton and ran through fairly flat country to Witney and then on westwards to Fairford. Let us descend in our balloon to the old town of Witney, famous for its blanket material since the thirteenth century. By the middle years of Queen Victoria's reign, the demand for blankets had become world-wide and the town's mills were finding it difficult and expensive to transport the goods.

In the early decades of the nineteenth century there were proposals to extend the Stratford to Moreton-in-Marsh horse tramway as far south as Witney, and on to the Thames at Eynsham. In 1836, there was a grandiose plan for a railway from the London and Birmingham at Tring, in the Hertfordshire Chilterns, across the Vale of Aylesbury to Oxford, and then, via Witney and Cirencester, to Cheltenham. However, it was after the building of the 'Old Worse and Worse' line from Oxford through Handborough and Charlbury, that Witney merchants were at last able to use a railway for their goods. A profitable carrier service was set up by William Payne, who carried vast loads of blankets, woollen goods and gloves made in Witney to the OW&WR line at Handborough.

It was the Early family, one of the chief mill owners in the town who promoted, with other businessmen, the Oxfordshire & Witney Railway in 1858. They had somewhat wider aspirations than some branch line promoters of their day and saw Witney as an important half-way point on a railway that would one day run westwards to Fairford and Cheltenham. The Oxford to Witney line received Royal Assent on 1 August 1859 and construction work began in May 1860, starting at Eynsham.

There was a traditional cutting of the first sod ceremony, the earth being deposited in a ceremonial wheelbarrow. The engineer for the new line was the famous Sir Charles Fox. Work proceeded quickly, so that the first passenger train ran on 13 November 1861. Goods traffic was fully in operation by 1 March 1862 after the goods shed at Witney was completed. As one might expect, the official opening day was declared a public holiday in Witney and the town was decorated with flags. The school children marched to the new terminus station and were given buns and oranges. But it was late in the season and the rain fell in torrents, yet despite it all, everyone enjoyed themselves. The official opening train arrived at 2pm, hauled by a West Midland Railway locomotive, (successors to the OW&WR). The Church bells were rung and bands played. An ox was duly 'cremated' and provided a rather tough and sooty meal to a vast crowd of 'artisans and labourers'. A somewhat more civilized feast was given at the Marlborough Arms for the middle and upper class guests.

The original promoters of the line were determined to make further progress and on 7 August of the same year, the East Gloucestershire Railway Act was passed. The line was planned to run through to Lechlade, Fairford, Andoversford, Withington, to Cheltenham. There was also a proposal to link with the GWR branch at Farringdon, south of the Thames valley. Lady Russell, wife of the new railway's Chairman, carried out the official cutting of the first sod ceremony amid rather boisterous crowds in a field near Cheltenham, on 31 March 1865. Work began on the embankments to take the line up to Dowdeswell and the Cotswold edge. Then the financial backing gave out and the northern end of the project was abandoned, although part of the earthworks was later used for the Banbury-Cheltenham railway.

Fortunately, enough money was forthcoming to enable work to go ahead in May 1869 on the extension from Witney to Fairford. This was completed in 1873. Stations were built between Witney and Fairford at Bampton (later re-named Brize Norton), Alvescot, and Lechlade. the old Witney station became a goods warehouse, the replacement station being on what was now the 'main' line. The branch was absorbed by the Great Western Railway on 1 July 1890. But even at this late date there were still hopes that Witney would be on a real main line railway. There were proposals for a London & South Wales Railway from London via Uxbridge, Beaconsfield, Wycombe, Bledlow and Oxford. The scheme was supported by the

Midland, L&NWR and Manchester, Sheffield and Lincolnshire (later GCR) railways. But the project was successfully blocked by the Great Western.

In 1906, the Fairford line was the first to be equipped with the GWR Automatic Train Control System. Traffic on the line was fairly light even in the First World War. It was not until the end of the 1930s and the threat of the Second World War that there came about a number of improvements. The establishment of air bases in the area brought much traffic. At Brize Norton, the runways actually crossed the line and special arrangements were made between the signal box and the control tower to stop trains when the aircraft were using the runway. A station was

opened at nearby Carterton on 2 October 1944, to serve the air base and also the sprawling civilian 'garden city' founded by William Carter before 1914. Presumably the early residents had to walk to Bampton (Brize Norton) or rely on the pioneer bus services. War materials passed along in an endless procession of trains and extra passing loops and tracks were laid down. Thousands of troops used the trains and the branch became a vital link in the war effort. There was even talk of a revival of the westward extension proposal, to provide a line through to the M&SWJR at Cirencester, or south to the Highworth terminus of the line from Swindon. But the war ended before anything was done.

The final years of the section from Witney to Fairford were typical of so many old Cotswold railways. The years of declining passengers; the weeds slowly taking over the platforms and sidings; the amount of goods traffic going down each year. Soon, only a handful of stalwart passengers braved the rainy lanes to the dimly lit stations. Nobody was really surprised when the Fairford section was closed completely on 18 June 1962. The Oxford to Witney passenger trains ceased at the same time. Goods trains continued but there was a touch of irony when British Railways itself suggested that Messrs Early should send their blanket products to Oxford by road instead of rail. Coal survived a little longer and the last train ran in November 1970.

Witney
The man strolling idly in the deserted street doesn't seem to be worried about traffic. But perhaps he should be, for just at the side of the Marlborough Arms (on the left) is the brand new sign 'Garage', and Witney is about to find itself in the age of solid-tyred motors.

Witney
Blanket Day at Witney goods yard just after the First World War. For many years the great London stores used to place bulk orders with Early and the other manufacturers ready for the winter trade. Special trains were run to Paddington – this one in immaculate condition is about to be pulled out of the yard by a Dean locomotive (No. 3247) and all the station staff have come out to see it off. The posters on the vehicles were an excellent publicity idea for Maples, the GWR and Early's Blankets.

Witney
Inside the mills of Charles Early & Co the blanket manufacturers. This picture was taken by the celebrated photographer Henry Taunt of Oxford in 1898.

The Hill. Witney.

Witney
Busy scene in Edwardian days, the crowd is descending from the Oxford train – perhaps to a special event in town. The locomotive is one of the GWR 'Metro' tanks, which were located at Oxford.

Witney
Busy scene on a summer's day as east and west trains cross. There are many traditional features of the Edwardian railway scene: milk churns; young ladies in their best dresses and smart station staff and buildings. The locomotive is a GWR 'Metro' tank.

Witney
Rural stations took great pride in their appearance and the station staff (including the dog) pose for the photographer one fine summer day in 1905.

Brize Norton and Bampton
Originally called just Bampton, a town in Oxfordshire not far from the line. The name was changed to Bampton (Oxon) and then Brize Norton, to avoid confusion with Bampton, Devon. Brize Norton Air Base was opened in 1937 and during the war became of great importance and the station was very heavily used.

Lechlade

Many famous personalities used this delighful rural station with its well kept flower beds, when they went to visit William Morris the poet and author who lived at nearby Kelmscott Manor. He died in London but his body was brought to this station on 3 October 1896. It was carried on a traditional Oxfordshire farm wagon to be buried at Kelmscott.

In 1935 a GWR advertisement stated:

LECHLADE

Road motor omnibuses of the Bristol Tramways & Carriage Co and the Midland 'Red' operate between Lechlade, Swindon and Banbury stations.

The observant will note that the signal box is in an unusual position, halfway down the platform.

Fairford

Although being the terminus of the East Gloucestershire line, the station layout was such that the goods yard lay beyond the passenger station and there was provision for expansion if the railway was ever extended westward. Indeed, there were plans even in the Second World War for a useful link to either the Swindon-Highworth branch or the Midland & South Western Junction line near Cirencester. By 1962, the flow of passengers was down to a few a day and services ceased.

Road train

This extraordinary vehicle was an early attempt to provide a road feeder service for the East Gloucestershire Railway. It ran westward to the M&SWJR at Andoversford. The front vehicle could carry up to three tons of parcels, with the trailer vehicle holding 20 people. The 'locomotive' was constructed by the Liquid Fuel Engineering Co of Cowes, I. of W. The service ran from 1898-9, being replaced by horse buses the following summer.

Fairford

It must have been a bumpy and noisy ride on this steam bus which connected the Fairford Terminus to Cirencester. The service began on 26 November 1904 and was operated by Nash of Lechlade. Note the driving chain to the heavy rear wheels. The vehicle had a water tank of 40 gallons capacity and this was refilled at Lechlade and Cirencester. The steam buses lasted until 1907.

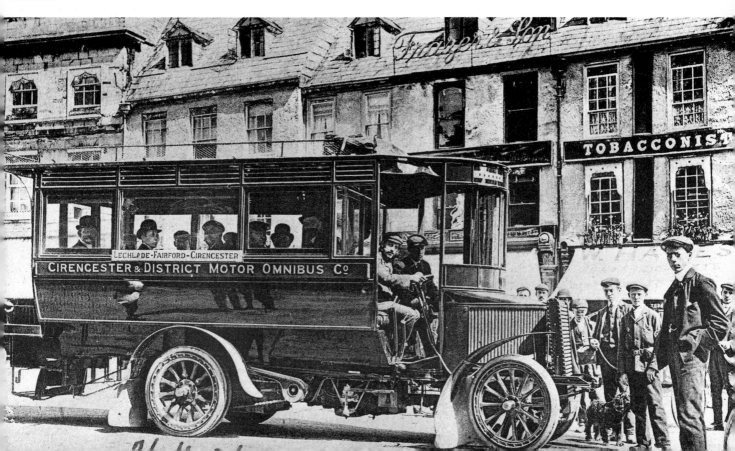

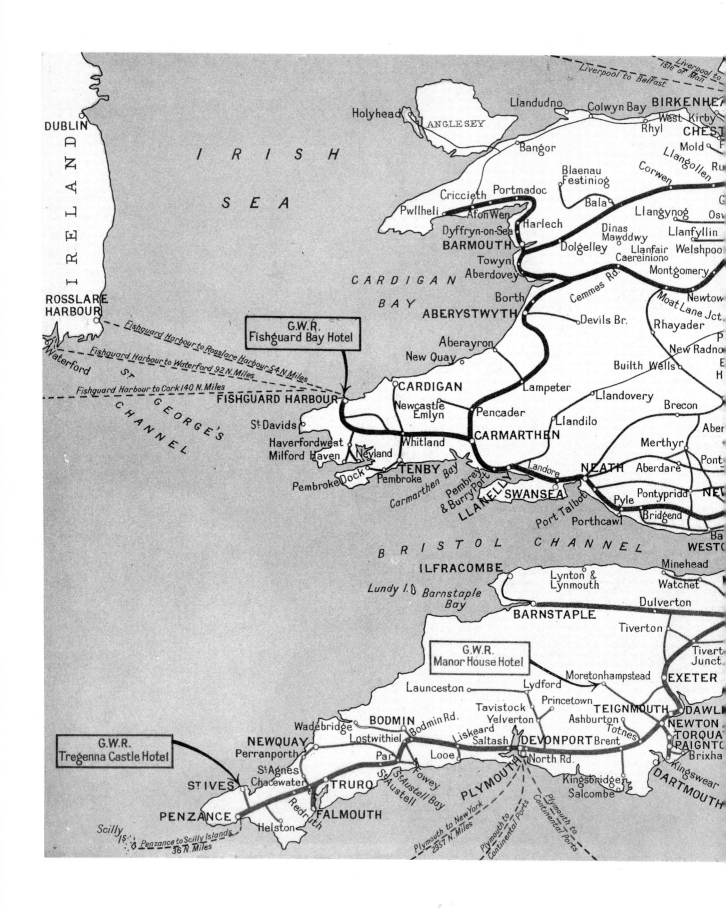